I would exhort you that ye deny not

the power of God; for he worketh by power,

according to the faith of the children of men, the same

today and tomorrow, and forever.

—MORONI 10:7

GOD

WANTS A

POWERFUL
PEOPLE

GOD
WANTS A
POWERFUL
PEOPLE

SHERI DEW

**DESERET
BOOK**

SALT LAKE CITY, UTAH

Photos on page xiv, 48, 60, and 92 courtesy of Getty Images; photo on page 22 courtesy of John Luke; photo on page 114 courtesy of Laurie Cook; photo on page 138 courtesy of Izak M. Taylor; photo on page 166 courtesy of Don Busath.

DESERET BOOK is a registered trademark of Deseret Book Company.

Visit us at DeseretBook.com

Library of Congress Cataloging-in-Publication Data

Dew, Sheri L.
  God wants a powerful people / Sheri Dew.
      p. cm.
  Includes bibliographical references and index.
  ISBN 978-1-59038-813-6 (hardback : alk. paper)
  1. Christian life—Mormon authors. 2. Power (Christian theology)
I. Title.
  BX8656.D465 2007
  248.4'89332—dc22   2007033497

Printed in the United States of America
Publishers Printing, Salt Lake City, UT

10   9   8   7   6   5   4   3   2   1

To Chayten, Mackley, Emma,
and all to follow in their generation

CONTENTS

INTRODUCTION

Several years ago I included a chapter entitled "God Wants a Powerful People" in another work, and also allowed a version of that message to be released as a talk on CD. Since that time, I have continued to ponder this theme—hence the expanded treatment in this book. Further, to set the stage for what follows, I have incorporated some of the material from that original chapter into the first few chapters of this book.

The words in this book are significant only insofar as they teach truth. The examples and stories are meant to do just one thing—show in practical ways how the gospel can change us, mold us, purify us, and sanctify us. What is far more significant than any words in print is what the Spirit will speak to your mind and heart as you read and ponder these doctrinal truths.

The reason to study and learn is so that we will change and do something, perhaps several somethings, differently from how we've done them before. So, as you read this book, I invite you to listen as the Spirit speaks to your mind and to your heart, identifying those things you ought to start doing or stop doing, do a little more or a little less of. The Holy Ghost is the Great Revelator and Translator, and He will reveal and translate truths in such a way that you can hear them, understand them, and apply them—all so that you will continue to progress and grow and change. Perhaps you will choose to reflect at the end of each chapter on something you can and perhaps should do differently. With the hope of being helpful, I'll suggest questions along the way to consider. But the most relevant questions for you will come as prompted by the Holy Ghost.

And we ask thee, Holy Father, that thy servants
may go forth from this house armed with thy power, and that thy
name may be upon them, and thy glory be round about them,
and thine angels have charge over them.

—DOCTRINE AND COVENANTS 109:22

We have a sacred obligation to seek after the power of God and then to use that power as He directs.

CHAPTER ONE

GOD WANTS A POWERFUL PEOPLE

While I was serving in the Relief Society general presidency, the Church instituted a new security system that required Church employees, general officers, and others who frequented the extended Church campus in downtown Salt Lake City—meaning Temple Square and the blocks housing the Conference Center and the Church Administration Building—to wear identification badges. This new system was implemented prior to the 2002 Winter Olympic Games, held in Salt Lake City just a few months before our presidency's release. Because we had served five years and were therefore easily recognized around Church headquarters, we rarely had much cause to use the ID badges. So I didn't develop the habit of wearing mine, though I usually carried it with me.

In the Saturday session of the April 2002 general conference, our presidency was released. We came and went to

1

sessions of that conference in the manner typical for General Authorities and general officers of the Church—meaning, we went to and from the Conference Center through a series of tunnels that connect the various buildings on the Church campus.

I had agreed to speak at an early-morning devotional for all Church hosts and hostesses serving in the Conference Center, Tabernacle, and other Church campus buildings. I was to be at the Little Theater in the Conference Center at 6:00 A.M. on the Sunday morning of general conference. As I drove to the Conference Center in the early morning, it dawned on me that the doors located at certain points along the tunnel might not be open that early.

Sure enough, the very first door in the tunnel was still locked. Wondering what to do, I noticed a buzzer by an intercom next to the large double doors. I pushed the buzzer, alerting a Church Security officer, identified who I was, explained my assignment in the Little Theater, and asked if he would let me through the door. "Sister Dew, do you have your ID badge with you?" he asked. When I rummaged through my binder and found it, the officer responded, "Your badge gives you access to all of these doors. Didn't you know that?"

"No," I admitted. "How do I use it?"

"Just hold it in front of the sensor, and the doors will open," the security officer instructed. Sure enough, as I waved the badge next to the sensor, *Voila!* the heavy security doors swung wide open.

"Cool!" I exclaimed, probably giving the officer an

early-morning chuckle. "You mean, I've been carrying with me all this time a badge that would give me entrance to all of these places on the Church campus, and I didn't even know it?"

"Yes," he said, then, quickly bringing me down to earth, continued, "And didn't you just get released, Sister Dew?" When I replied yes, he said, "Well, enjoy the badge today, because tomorrow it will be deactivated."

Just as he promised, all of the doors through the tunnel sprang open in *Open Sesame!* fashion as I held my badge in front of the sensor next to each of them. And, also just as he predicted, the next day the card no longer worked. The privilege was gone.

The irony was unmistakable. For months I had carried with me a badge that had given me privileges I hadn't understood or, worse, taken advantage of. I had not understood that badge's power.

For months I had carried with me a badge that had given me privileges I hadn't understood or, worse, taken advantage of. I had not understood that badge's power.

I couldn't help but think about Dorothy in *The Wizard of Oz*, who went to extraordinary lengths to find the Wizard because she believed he had the power to help her get back home to Kansas. It was not until after she'd made an exhausting, unfruitful journey that she learned she'd had the power with her all along to get back home—power contained in the ruby red slippers she'd been wearing.

We are all trying to find our way back home—and I don't

mean just to Kansas. And we seem to look anywhere and everywhere *in the world*—to "experts" in all their glory—for clues on how to get there. We look for ways to increase our skills and talents, enhance our gifts, expand our influence, improve our lot in life, and find happiness. But the truth is that the Lord has already given His people—covenanted, faithful, believing Saints—everything they need to find their way back home. Many of those Saints have already received the gift of the Holy Ghost. Many have been ordained and hold the priesthood of God. Many are walking around with the most precious recommendation of all, a "badge" that gives them entrance to the Lord's House, which is a house of glory wherein they are endowed with power. Many have entered the new and everlasting covenant of marriage, which affords them even greater blessings, privileges, and power.

To return to *The Wizard of Oz*, recall for a moment the scene where the Wicked Witch is melting. As she disappears, she exclaims to and about Dorothy, "Oh, what a world, what a world. Who would have thought a good little girl like you could destroy all my beautiful wickedness!"

Good little boys and girls, meaning covenant-making men and women, filled with the power of God, are perfectly poised to destroy the beautiful wickedness so evident in our world. I was reminded of this a few weeks ago, when I joined members of our extended family at the Salt Lake International Airport to greet a nephew returning from his mission. Because there were about a dozen returning elders on his flight, which had originated in Mexico, and also because it happened to be the evening of the Fourth of July, the airport was jam-packed with families, banners, American flags, red-white-and-blue balloons, *Welcome Home* and *Bienvenidos a Casa* signs, cameras, and nervous fathers and mothers easy to spot because they were all on the verge of tears. As we caught the first sight of our missionary, tears started to flow all around. After serving honorably and well and doing what he'd been commissioned to do, he was home. It seemed so long ago and yet almost like yesterday that we'd said good-bye for a season.

He first hugged his mother, who was instantly in a puddle. Then his father, who held him in an embrace that of itself said, *Well done.* Then his sister just older than he, who herself had recently returned from the mission field. And then of course there were hugs and smiles and tears and flashing cameras coming from all directions. Pictures with his parents, with his sisters, with his brother, with his cousins, with just about anyone and everyone within reach. You know the scene.

As the happy scene unfolded, I thought that there may be few experiences in mortality that more closely resemble or approximate what it may be like when we ultimately return Home. Here, grateful parents, family members, and friends, almost giddy with excitement, gather to greet the young man or woman who's been away from home on a mission for a season. Letters, weekly e-mails, and two phone calls a year have maintained contact, though at a minimum and requiring far more effort than before. It's been a glorious time, a hard time, and a time of immeasurable growth for the missionary. Though the parents in particular have missed their son or daughter, they also realize they couldn't have provided at home the kind of experience he or she was having—and needed to have—in the full-time service of the Lord, where lessons in consecration, obedience, prayer, sacrifice, faith, testimony, and sheer endurance have been plentiful, constant, and often life-changing.

As my nephew hugged one person after another, there were many to celebrate his return and share in the joy of all he had experienced and accomplished. We had all had complete faith in him—not only in the kind of young man he was, but in the kind of missionary service he would render. He had been elated to enter the mission field and had never looked back. Upon his return, he was so filled with light that it seemed clear he'd kept himself clean. His soles with holes, the third such pair, were evidence (among others) that he'd worked hard helping bring souls to Christ. And God had blessed and protected him.

We left the airport just as the last faint light of dusk faded into nighttime. Because it was the night of the Fourth, we drove home to the sight of fireworks cascading all along the Wasatch Front. The fireworks seemed so appropriate on that evening, not just to celebrate the birth and freedom of our nation, but to mark the triumphant return of a young missionary who had done what he said he would do.

Missions are all about change. Missions change men and women.

Our mission on earth is designed to change us. It is designed to transform us. It was planned to give us the chance to be wise even though separated from the presence of our

Father, to strip ourselves of uncleanness, to refuse to yield to temptation, and to choose *not* to consume our probation upon our lusts but to serve the true and living God (see Mormon 9:28).

Happily, we are not expected to endure or experience this mission alone. From the top of the heavens, our Heavenly Father and His Son have sent and continue to send their love and their blessing, not to mention guidance when we seek it. Surely the ancients who foresaw our day, and the heavenly hosts, count-

Our mission on earth is designed to change us. It is designed to transform us.

less numbers of them, cheer us on, pray for us, empathize with our anguish, and find joy in all we accomplish, overcome, and endure. Clearly our Father and His Son have faith in our abilities—or They wouldn't have sent us now. Thus, it is for us to keep ourselves clean, meaning pure and holy before Them, and to demonstrate by our actions and choices that we want to be part of the kingdom of God more than we want anything else.

That is our charge and our quest. The question for us is, How will we do it?

On June 13, 2004, the Manhattan New York Temple was dedicated. As is customary, prior to that dedication, in May, an open house was held in which thousands of Latter-day Saints as well as people not of our faith toured the beautiful new temple located kitty-corner from New York City's famous Lincoln Center, home to the Metropolitan Opera. I had the privilege of participating as a guide during the VIP open houses, and in New York City VIP week was just that—VIP week—drawing the Big Apple's *glitterati* from the worlds of journalism, finance, business, politics, and the media.

Considering the array of celebrities who had expressed an interest in touring the temple—and particularly journalists who would be likely to quote anything they heard—I assumed those of us serving as hosts and hostesses would be trained on the best way to handle the questions that would inevitably arise. Our training, though, was simple and consisted largely of a few suggestions about how to best explain what takes place in the temple and why it is central to all we believe. In addition, though, we were taught one guiding principle. "When all is said and done," we were told, "you'll want to say as little as possible, because God likes to do His own teaching in His own House."

That week I repeatedly witnessed that truth in action. When someone was touched during a tour, it had nothing to do with the host or hostess and everything to do with the Spirit of the Lord resting upon and communicating with that individual's spirit. It is a magnificent pattern that governs all heavenly teaching. Indeed, the Lord likes to do His own teaching through ministrations and revelations of the Holy Ghost. It is the Holy Ghost who converts, teaches,

The Lord likes to do His own teaching through ministrations and revelations of the Holy Ghost.

and inspires. It is the Holy Ghost and His power that moves us, impressing ideas and concepts upon our hearts and minds that we've never thought about before or even believed, changing us over time. It is the Holy Ghost who reveals the Father's will, who comforts and has the capacity to bring a change of heart more complete and transforming than anything this world has to offer. It is the Holy Ghost who is the Divine Translator and Revelator and who makes it possible for us to receive instructions from our Father.

We speak often of the gift of the Holy Ghost, but Nephi learned in his vision of the latter days that the Holy Ghost is a gift of pure power (see 1 Nephi 13:37). He gives us the power to feel peace, comfort, and reassurance even when circumstances in life are not peaceful, comforting, or reassuring. The power to speak a language, even the language of revelation, that only He is authorized to teach. The power to part the veil and commune with the heavens. The power to be transformed and changed, and even to put off the natural man and become "submissive, meek, humble, patient, full of love, willing to submit to all things which the Lord seeth fit to inflict upon [us]" (Mosiah 3:19). The power to become like our Father and His Only Begotten Son.

Fulfilling and completing a successful mission is no small thing. Just ask any returned missionary. Likewise, successfully fulfilling our mortal probation, our mission on earth, is a tall order for those selected to live in what is surely the most complex time in the history of the earth. This rite of passage we refer to as mortality can sometimes feel like nothing short of a spook alley. Prophets, seers, and revelators have repeatedly likened our day to that of Sodom and Gomorrah. Sadly, our day seems to have at least equaled if not exceeded that sobering time in ancient history when depravity and evil ran amok. Our day seems unbelievably complicated when we consider that the most blatant evil the world has to offer is available to us 24/7 and can even be downloaded instantly to our cell phones, if we choose. Such constant access and exposure to evil and evil-doing unfortunately breeds familiarity, then tolerance, followed by begrudging acceptance, and finally endorsement.

Should this discourage us? President Gordon B. Hinckley says no. He has been heard to say that the only thing he regrets about his life is that his advanced age will prevent him from seeing everything that is going to occur between now and the time the Lord comes again. That is not the outlook of a frightened, pessimistic leader.

"Perilous times?" he asked rhetorically in a general conference address. "Yes. These are perilous times. But the human race has lived in peril from the time before the earth was created. Somehow, through all of the darkness, there has been a faint but beautiful light. And now with added luster it shines upon the world. It carries with it God's plan of happiness for His children. It carries with it the great and unfathomable wonders of the Atonement of the Redeemer. How grateful we are to the God of heaven for His beneficent care of His children in providing for them, through all of the perils of eternity, the opportunity of salvation and the blessing of exaltation in

His kingdom, if only they will live in righteousness" ("The Dawning of a Brighter Day," 83).

President Hinckley continued by quoting Wilford Woodruff: " 'The Almighty is with this people. We shall have all the revelations that we will need, if we will do our duty and obey the commandments of God. . . . Let us fill our mission'" ("The Dawning of a Brighter Day," 83).

In this dispensation, prophets have repeatedly reaffirmed that if we are prepared both temporally and spiritually, just as Captain Moroni prepared his people temporally and spiritually (see Alma 48:7–10), then we need not fear either the day in which we live or the future.

God wants a powerful people, and He has made it possible for us to have access to His power, for He never intended us to face the perils of mortality alone, having only our own strength, wisdom, and power to draw upon.

Two comforting concepts can help dispel our fears about mortality. First, we can know that we are here now because we are supposed to be here now, and we came trailing clouds of glory, fully prepared for the unique challenges and complexities we would face in the latter part of the latter days. Second, we can understand that God wants a powerful people, and He has made it possible for us to have access to His power, for He never intended us to face the perils of mortality alone, having only our own strength, wisdom, and power to draw upon.

Not long ago I was preparing a Sunday School lesson on chapters from the book of Isaiah for a group of high school juniors and seniors. The challenge, of course, was to make Isaiah's teachings relevant for these bright and faithful but squirmy young men and women. While I was studying several classic Isaiah passages, all of which contained prophecies regarding our day, it dawned on me that when ancient prophets prophesied, they almost universally prophesied about two major things. First and foremost, they taught that Jesus Christ was the Son of God, that He would come to the world, that He would offer up an infinite and eternal sacrifice, that He is our Savior and our Redeemer. The second subject about which almost every ancient prophet prophesied is the Last Days—in other words, us. Search the writings of Isaiah or Jeremiah or Daniel, Mormon or Nephi or Moroni, the Apostle Paul—select *any* ancient prophet. They all testified of Christ, and nearly all of them foresaw our day and prophesied about what would come during the dispensation of the fulness of times.

Imagine! From the time Adam and Eve left the Garden of Eden and began their pioneering sojourn as our mortal parents, our Father has sent prophets to the earth. And He has inspired them to prophesy and testify of two things: Jesus Christ, and us.

Do you think there is any chance the Lord would have inspired His prophets to prophesy about us, only to then take a chance on the outcome of the latter days by sending men and women He couldn't count on? There is no chance—*zero chance*—He would have done that. President George Q. Cannon taught that "God has reserved . . . choice spirits to come forth in this last dispensation, because of the greatness and the magnitude of the work to be accomplished. . . . It has required apparently the most valiant men and women to come forth in the last days . . . [because] this is not a short lived dispensation; it is to go on increasing in power . . . until it shall fill the whole earth. . . . And, of course, it requires great valor, great obedience and great gifts in order to accomplish the end that is to be attained under the promises of God. The Lord has permitted spirits to be born among the various races of mankind that are fitted and qualified to accomplish this great work" (*Gospel Truth*, 18).

There is, however, a sobering reality attached to this grand truth: We may have been chosen to come to earth now, but our foreordination is not a guarantee. It is an indication of profound, divine confidence. But it is not a guarantee. And thus, foreordination is not enough. Just as a missionary must, every day of his mission, determine how hard he will work and how sincerely he will plead with the Spirit to guide him, we must choose every day of our mortal missions whom we will follow and whom we will serve in this most arduous of times.

We may have been chosen to come to earth now, but our foreordination is not a guarantee. It is an indication of profound, divine confidence. But it is not a guarantee.

So during this complex, confusing, complicated, joyous, adventurous, growing, hand-wringing, sanctifying time called mortality, how will we manage to do what we came here to do? How will we avoid the distractions and darts of the adversary, the pits and pitfalls strewn along our path?

For the last days are not for the faint of heart or the spiritually out of shape. There will be days when we feel defeated, exhausted, and plain old beat-up by life's whiplash. People we love will disappoint us— and we will disappoint them. We'll almost certainly struggle with some kind of physical appetite, and perhaps several. Some days it will feel as though the veil between heaven and earth is made of reinforced concrete. And we may even face a crisis of faith. In fact, we can *count* on experiencing trials that will test our testimony, our obedience, and our faith—because how do we know if we really have a testimony, if we'll really obey, if we really want to be honest and chaste and virtuous, and if we really believe in Jesus Christ, if those things aren't put to the test?

How do we know if we really have a testimony, if we'll really obey, if we really want to be honest and chaste and virtuous, and if we really believe in Jesus Christ, if those things aren't put to the test?

I have learned in recent years, in ways I never would have anticipated, that none of us are beyond the reach of fear and pain and disappointment so intense that it can threaten, if even just for a short time, our testimony and faith.

Lest this seem too negative a thought about our lives and our future, I hasten to add that I am nothing if not optimistic about our time here in mortality. Everything about our lives is an indicator of our Father's respect for us, that He *recommended* and *selected* us for now, when the stakes are so high, when His kingdom is being established once and for all, never again to be taken from the earth. He chose us to run the last leg of the relay, when He needs His strongest, fittest runners. He believes in us.

The simple fact is that our Father did not recommend Sarah or Moses or Nephi or countless other magnificent exemplars for this dispensation. He recommended you and me. A common theme of patriarchal blessings given to our youth these days is that they were sent now because our Father's most trustworthy children would be needed in the final, decisive battle for righteousness.

Two recent events demonstrated how true this is. As the Young Women in our ward prepared for girls camp this summer, the Laurels asked which days I would be at camp. "When should I come?" I responded. Their answer was immediate: "Come on Friday, that's the best day. It's the 'spiritual day' when we have testimony meeting." It *was* a great day, and as they bore their testimonies, their breadth and depth of spirit was apparent in what they said as well as in the presence of the Spirit throughout.

Then, a few days later, when I asked a teenage niece who had just returned from EFY how it was, she said, "I loved it! It was so great!"

"What did you like the best?" I asked.

Her response was immediate: "Thursday. That's the spiritual day when we wear Sunday clothes and bear our testimonies and stuff."

For all the traps Satan sets constantly for our youth, and for all their temptation with the world's glitz and glamour, it is telling that what they actually love most is *feeling* the Spirit. The rising generation is the finest this world has ever seen. Period. I've met too many of them in too many parts of the world to ever convince me otherwise. I've felt the overwhelming witness of the Spirit that comes into groups large and small of young adults and teenagers. This is simply who our youth are, and it is who they have always been.

> *The rising generation is the finest this world has ever seen. Period. . . . This is simply who our youth are, and it is who they have always been.*

So, how will we and the youth we are mentioning live up to our Father's recommendation? Happily, though we must each walk through life on our own, we don't have to do it alone. Here are four principles to consider:

First, God wants a powerful people. He wants a people who know and learn what Ammon knew and learned, that in "his strength," meaning the strength of God, they "can do all things" (Alma 26:12).

Second, He gives His power to those who are faithful and who qualify.

Third, we therefore have a sacred obligation to seek after the power of God and then to use that power as He directs. There can't be many things more disheartening to our Father than when we, His children, refuse the gifts He's offered us. In a revelation outlining the characteristics of those who would inherit the celestial, terrestrial, and telestial kingdoms, the Lord explained that we would ultimately be allowed to "enjoy that which they are willing to receive, because they were not willing to enjoy that which they *might have received.* For what doth it profit a man if a gift is bestowed upon him, and he receive not the gift? Behold, he rejoices not in that which is given unto him, neither rejoices in him who is the giver of the gift" (D&C 88:32–33; emphasis added). Thus, we are obligated to seek after the power God has offered the righteous, and are foolish if we don't.

And fourth, when we have the power of God with us, nothing is impossible.

God wants a powerful people, and there are countless evidences of this fact. At baptism, which can occur as early as age eight, we become eligible to receive the gift and power of the Holy Ghost and thus the privilege of constant access to the third member of the Godhead.

Imagine, an eight-year-old may receive this remarkable gift!

Twelve-year-old boys may be ordained to the Aaronic Priesthood, which holds "the key of the ministering of angels and the preparatory gospel; Which gospel is the gospel of repentance and of baptism and the remission of sins" (D&C 84:26–27).

Every adult who qualifies may enter the House of the Lord, where he or she may "grow up" in the Lord—consider the implications of that metaphor—and "receive a fulness of the Holy Ghost" (D&C 109:15). Further, those who emerge from the temple do so surrounded and protected by God's power (see D&C 109:22). Elder Bruce R. McConkie explained that "'the fulness of the priesthood' is received only in the temple itself. This fulness is received through washings, anointings, solemn assemblies, oracles in holy places, conversations, ordinances, endowments, and sealings. (D&C 124:40.) It is in the temple that we enter into the patriarchal order, the order of priesthood that bears the name 'the new and everlasting covenant of marriage'" (*A New Witness for the Articles of Faith*, 315). Thus, when two people enter the new and everlasting covenant of marriage, they have additional privileges and power sealed upon them as a couple.

In a multitude of ways, the Lord has made it clear that He desires to have a righteous, pure people who both qualify for and seek to have access to His power.

God has endowed His people with power because He loves us, yearns for us to return home, and knows full well that only

> *In a multitude of ways, the Lord has made it clear that He desires to have a righteous, pure people who both qualify for and seek to have access to His power.*

with His help—and drawing upon His power—may we expect to complete our missions well and return to His loving, grateful, welcoming arms.

Elder Richard L. Evans, a member of the Quorum of the Twelve from 1953 to 1971, told a group of youth that "it is good to be faithful. But how much better it is to be faithful and competent" (as quoted in Hafen, *The Broken Heart*, 91). Our quest is certainly to be faithful, but it is also to learn as much as we can, become as knowledgeable as we can be—both in what we study and what we're taught by the Spirit—so that we know *how* to qualify for and gain access to the power of the Lord. The influence of all who learn this increases manyfold.

Who hasn't dropped a pebble in a still pool of water and watched the rippling effect as the force of that one small rock ripples on and on? Metaphors surrounding water are plentiful.

God has endowed His people with power because He loves us, yearns for us to return home, and knows full well that only with His help—and drawing upon His power—may we expect to complete our missions well and return to His loving, grateful, welcoming arms.

The North Shore on the island of Oahu in Hawaii is not only breathtakingly beautiful, but there is a feeling and spirit permeating the area in and around Laie, home to

BYU—Hawaii, the Polynesian Cultural Center, and the Laie Hawaii Temple, the fifth operating temple in this dispensation and the first outside of Utah (not counting Kirtland and Nauvoo).

Who hasn't dropped a pebble in a still pool of water and watched the rippling effect as the force of that one small rock ripples on and on?

There is a place on the North Shore, not far from Laie, where the view of the vast Pacific as it rolls toward shore is something to behold. Wave after wave comes rolling in from an ocean that seems to stretch on forever. Many times I have stood on that beach and watched an endless sequence of whitecaps roll to the shore, crashing against rocks and beach as they hit land.

During the winter months, the waves along the North Shore are among the largest in the world, but during other seasons they seem almost tame as they roll in from the Pacific—until they crash against rocks and beach, at which point their power is undeniable. Further, the waves never stop.

The metaphor of that scene is vivid. I have imagined wave after wave after wave of righteous men and women, endowed with the power of God, stepping forward to take their place in the battle between right and wrong. When that power crashes up against evil, its force is undeniable.

We comprise those waves of followers who have been sent in the eleventh hour to do all we can to build up the kingdom of God. The Lord has given us, through membership in the Church, a badge of sorts, a card that not only identifies us as His followers but grants us privileges and holy power. For, as Elder Bruce R. McConkie said, "*Whenever* the Lord has a people on earth, he endows them with power from on high" (*A New Witness for the Articles of Faith*, 363). Those who come to understand how to use this power will in very fact come in waves—waves that never end—to help destroy the "beautiful wickedness" of the world by building up the kingdom of God.

*If we were born to lead in these latter days (and we were),
then we need to understand how God makes His power available
to us, what it takes to qualify to receive that
power, and how we gain access to that power.*

CHAPTER TWO

HOW GOD SHARES HIS POWER

G od wants a powerful people. No one understands better than He that Satan is real and has, according to the Prophet Joseph Smith, "marvelous power" (JS–H 1:16). No one better understands how complex and filled with booby traps the mortal experience is. No one better understands that none of us are smart or resilient enough to spar with Satan and survive spiritually. The adversary is a snake in the grass, lying in wait not only to deceive but to strike and, if possible, spiritually poison and even kill.

I live in the foothills that surround Salt Lake City, and during this most recent hot summer one neighbor after another mentioned finding snakes in their yards. I HATE SNAKES! No, actually, I'm terrified of, even *traumatized* about, snakes. One by one, I told each neighbor with great relief that none of the slimy, disgusting reptiles had shown up in my yard. Until a few days later, there one was, stretched out in my backyard.

Other than dealing with my near cardiac arrest, what surprised me most was how hidden the creepy creature was. It had crawled into a little furrow in the lawn, and that, combined with its coloring, made it almost impossible to see. And yet there it was, waiting to strike at the next unsuspecting victim—which victim could have been me.

Snakes are a fitting metaphor for Satan and his tactics. Some are big, ugly, and hang from trees in a way that would be impossible to miss, but most varieties do a lot of hiding. They hide by blending in with their surroundings. They hide by slinking into cracks and crevices. Some signal before striking; others don't. But in certain kinds of environments, you can almost be sure that snakes are there.

Where there is any kind of dishonesty, immorality, contention, violence, perversion, or addiction, there is Satan.

By the same token, Satan is *everywhere* today, waiting to strike at his next victim. Where there is *any kind* of dishonesty, immorality, contention, violence, perversion, or addiction, there is Satan. He is in blatant sin; he is in subtle deception. Stay away from him. Satan is "a roaring lion, [who] walketh about, seeking whom he may devour" (1 Peter 5:8). And he will devour us—unless we "put on the whole armour [or power] of God, that [we] may be able to stand against the wiles of the devil" (Ephesians 6:11).

Thank heaven for the knowledge that there is a way to

withstand Lucifer, for his influence and power cannot be over-estimated or overstated. In vision Enoch "beheld Satan; and he had a great chain in his hand, and it veiled the whole face of the earth with darkness; and he looked up and laughed, and his angels rejoiced" (Moses 7:26). And in his own interchange with Lucifer, Moses experienced the wrath of hell. After Moses resisted Satan's temptations twice and commanded him to depart, "Satan cried with a loud voice, and ranted upon the earth. . . . And it came to pass that Moses began to fear exceedingly; and as he began to fear, he saw the bitterness of hell" (Moses 1:19–20). At that point Moses showed us how to deal with the adversary, in the process demonstrating the dramatic and sublime truth that the power of God is stronger than the power of Satan. The scriptures record this sequence of events:

"Nevertheless, calling upon God, he [Moses] received strength, and he commanded, saying: Depart from me, Satan, for this one God only will I worship, which is the God of glory. And now Satan began to tremble, and the earth shook; and Moses received strength, and called upon God, saying: In the name of the Only Begotten, depart hence, Satan. And it came to pass that Satan cried with a loud voice, with weeping, and wailing, and gnashing of teeth; and he departed hence, even from the presence of Moses, that he beheld him not" (Moses 1:20–22).

Satan was forced to depart, at which time Moses "lifted up his eyes unto heaven, being filled with the Holy Ghost, which beareth record of the Father and the Son; And calling upon the name of God, he beheld his glory again, for it was upon him; and he heard a voice, saying: Blessed art thou, Moses, for I, the Almighty, have chosen thee, and thou shalt be made stronger than many waters; for they shall obey thy command as if thou wert God" (Moses 1:24–25).

Consider what we learn from this account: first, that the power of God is greater than the power of Satan—*always*; second, that even though Satan frightened Moses, such that momentarily he saw the bitterness of hell, he called upon God, who strengthened him and clearly gave him access to His power; third, drawing upon that power, Moses banished Satan and was filled with the Holy Ghost; and finally, having had the faith to trust that God would deliver him, Moses was given access to even greater power, including the promise that he would be made "stronger than many waters," the fulfillment of which promise he received on the banks of the Red Sea. As Pharaoh's army later bore down upon the children of Israel, Moses didn't just magically part the Red Sea; long before then he had learned to trust in the power of God and had also learned how to access that power.

Indeed, the power of God and the power of Satan are as different as night and day, as different as truth and error or goodness and evil. Satan's power is temporary and will end (in fact, he's running out of time, and he knows it, which is why his devices are more desperate and extreme than ever before); God's power is absolute and endless. Satan uses his power to deceive, destroy, and damn; God uses His power to bless, sanctify, and exalt. Satan's arrogance blinds him as well as those who follow him; God is all-seeing and all-knowing. Satan abandons those he spiritually maims, while God has promised to make all of His faithful children "joint-heirs with Christ" (Romans 8:17) and to bless them with the "riches of eternity" (D&C 38:39).

There *is* one thing the power of God and the power of Satan have in common: Neither can influence us unless we allow them to. The devil can't *make us do anything.* Said the Prophet Joseph Smith: "Satan cannot seduce us by his enticements unless we in our hearts consent and yield" (Ehat and Cook, eds., *Words of Joseph Smith,* 65). On the other hand, although God could manipulate us, He never has and never will. We are free to "choose . . . eternal life, through the great Mediator of all men, or to choose captivity and death, according to the . . . power of the devil" (2 Nephi 2:27). *In short, the kind of power operating in our lives is entirely up to us.*

There is one thing the power of God and the power of Satan have in common: Neither can influence us unless we allow them to.

As it turns out, our Father is serious about agency—serious enough that in some respects and in many circumstances, our agency is allowed even to override His will. Imagine, He cared about us enough to provide us with a true test, a true probation—one in which we could actually make our own choices. We can choose to seek and follow His will, or we can do otherwise, as we please. To be sure, there are consequences to either route, with the one path leading back home to Him, and the other leading to eternal damnation or at the very least some degree of diminishment. Nonetheless, our Father has given us our agency to determine whom we will follow, how we will spend our time in mortality, and what kind of men and women we will become.

Said President Spencer W. Kimball to a group of young adults: "You are sent to this earth not merely to have a good time or to satisfy urges or passions or desires. You are sent to this earth, not to ride merry-go-rounds, airplanes, automobiles, and have what the world calls 'fun.' You are sent to this world with a very serious purpose. You are sent to school, for that matter, to begin as a human infant and grow to unbelievable proportions in wisdom, judgment, knowledge, and power" (*Teachings of Spencer W. Kimball*, 31).

Thus, if God wants a powerful people who can withstand the wiles of the devil here and eventually reign hereafter (and He does), and if we were born to lead in these latter days (and we were), then we need to understand how God makes His power available to us, what it takes to qualify to receive that power, and how we gain access to that power.

Here are *some* of the ways God makes His power available to us:

1. There is power in the word of God.

Alma and the sons of Mosiah learned that the preaching of the word—meaning the gospel of Jesus Christ—had a "great tendency to lead the people to do that which was just" and that it had a "more powerful effect upon the minds of the people than the sword, or anything else." Alma implored his people to "try the virtue of the word of God" (Alma 31:5). There is power in the word to heal our wounded souls (Jacob 2:8), to help us overcome temptation and come unto Christ (1 Nephi 11:25), to prompt us to repent (Jarom 1:12), to humble us (Alma 32:14), to help us overcome the natural man (Mosiah 3:19), to bring about a mighty change in our hearts (Alma 5:13), to bless us with revelation and the spirit of prophecy (Jacob 4:6), and to lead us to Christ.

President Boyd K. Packer taught that "true doctrine, understood, changes attitudes and behavior. The study of the doctrines of the gospel will improve behavior quicker than a study of behavior will improve behavior" ("Little Children," 17). In other words, the word of God can lead us to change. It can literally transform us. And it can be a primary means through which we receive personal revelation.

"*Words of doctrine [have] great power,*" said Elder Henry B. Eyring of the Quorum of the Twelve. "They can open the minds of people to see spiritual things not visible to the natural eye. And they can open the heart to feelings of the love of God and a love for truth. The Savior drew on both those sources of power, to open our eyes and open hearts" ("The Power of Teaching Doctrine," 73; emphasis added).

Thus, immersion in the word of God changes us. It transforms those who plumb its depths. It changes those who are just beginning to taste the sweetness of the goodness of God.

Not long ago I found myself seated next to a bright, young-adult-age woman on a cross-country flight. We struck up a casual conversation at first, but one that became more serious when she noticed scriptures among the materials I was reading. Noting that my scriptures looked different from hers, she asked about them, which led to a discussion about the Book of Mormon and the Restoration. Judging me at that point, I suppose, to be a safe sounding board, she asked if I had an opinion about the kinds of female role models so prevalent in our society today—particularly all of the celebrity "bad girls," as she referred to them. Soon we were discussing the plummeting moral standard among women, and at one point I had a perfect opening to tell her about the Relief Society and its members. That's when I pulled out of my scriptures a bookmark-size copy of the Relief Society Declaration that I always keep with me, handed it to her, and told her that this statement described the kind of women we were striving to become. As she read the Declaration, she became emotional. Finally, after regaining some composure, she said, "You mean, there are other women living like I'm trying to live?"

"Yes, about five million of them," I said, smiling.

She then started to ask specific questions about parts of the Declaration—doctrinal statements about who we are, our

Immersion in the word of God changes us. It transforms those who plumb its depths. It changes those who are just beginning to taste the sweetness of the goodness of God.

purpose in life, the power of the scriptures, and so forth. One question led to another, which led to one scripture after another, and by the time we landed she had committed to read the Book of Mormon. I don't know where she currently is in her quest, but I do know that as she read passages from the Book of Mormon for the first time, she said, "I can feel something from this book."

She was experiencing the power of the word.

It is the same power that changed the heart of a young adult girl who told me recently, "I always knew when we recited the Young Women theme every week that I was a daughter of God, and I believed it. Kind of. But one day it hit me like that ton of bricks you always hear about that I really was a daughter of God and I'd better find out what that meant, so I started reading the Book of Mormon again and it's just all so clear why I need to keep the commandments. If I REALLY am a daughter of God, and I know I am, then I'd better dress like one and act like one."

It is the power of the word, specifically power that came from reading the Book of Mormon after a prolonged absence from full activity in the Church, that prompted a lifelong friend, addicted to pornography, to begin the long and painful road back.

It is the power of the word that reached a young couple on the verge of divorce when they promised their bishop they would read the scriptures every day together.

It is the power of the word that converted a professor in a European university. When missionaries knocked on her door, she invited them in, pointed to her various Ph.D. diplomas hanging on the wall, one of which was in theology, then began to talk to the two young men (who hadn't even a fraction of the knowledge she had) about the study of religion. But she accepted the invitation to read the Book of Mormon and a couple of months later was baptized. She told those attending her baptism that the missionaries who had taught her were wonderful, but they hadn't converted her. Since the day she had met them, she had read the Book of Mormon, the Doctrine and Covenants, the Pearl of Great Price, all of James E. Talmage's writings, and several other volumes of Church doctrine.

Then she said, in words to this effect, "After years of studying philosophy, I picked up the D&C and read a few verses that answered some of the greatest questions of Aristotle and Socrates. When I read those verses, I wept." She concluded: "I don't think you know what you have. The world is starving for what you have. I am like a starving person being led to a feast. And over these eight and a half weeks I have been able to feast in a way I have never known possible."

Some may be skeptical about these kinds of transformations. But as Elder Eyring explained, "Doctrine gains its power as the Holy Ghost confirms that it is true" ("The Power of Teaching Doctrine," 74). Hence, the gospel has the power to cleanse, change, heal, and make new, because the word is "quick and powerful," it "divide[s] asunder all the cunning and the snares and the wiles of the devil," and it leads the man of Christ in a straight and narrow path away from the gulf of misery prepared by Satan to engulf the wicked (Helaman 3:29). The Atonement is real. My friends are evidence of that. Great change is the change that comes with conversion; it is the change that comes from immersing ourselves in doctrine.

Do we know what we believe? Do we know there is power in the doctrine of Christ to change and overcome weakness? Do we realize that the scriptures contain the answer to every life dilemma? Do we know enough about our doctrine to discern the skillful, even artful, packaging of transgression so blatant in the world today? A casual understanding of the gospel will not sustain us through the days ahead, which is why it is imperative that we immerse ourselves in the word of God.

In all of scripture, nowhere are the doctrines of the gospel more fully taught than in the Book of Mormon. The Prophet Joseph declared that "a man would get nearer to God by abiding by its precepts, than by any other book" (*History of the Church*, 4:461). Indeed, the Lord Himself endorsed this book, declaring, "He [meaning Joseph Smith] has translated the book, even that part which I have commanded him, and as your Lord and your God liveth it is true" (D&C 17:6). The ramifications of that declaration are resounding. For in His testimony of the veracity of the Book of Mormon, God

> *A casual understanding of the gospel will not sustain us through the days ahead, which is why it is imperative that we immerse ourselves in the word of God.*

Himself, as Elder Bruce R. McConkie explained, "laid his god-hood on the line. Either the book is true or God ceases to be God. There neither is nor can be any more formal or powerful language known to men or gods" ("The Doctrine of the Priesthood," 33).

It is significant that to commemorate the two hundredth anniversary of Joseph Smith's birth, President Hinckley invited all members of the Church to do one thing—read the Book of Mormon. Perhaps there is nothing the prophet could have done to infuse the Church as a whole with greater spirituality and power than to invite more than twelve million members to simultaneously join in reading, searching, and pondering the most spiritually penetrating of all books.

There is power in the word, for the Word is God. And the Word is persuasively taught in the Book of Mormon, which a latter-day prophet has promised will bring power into our lives.

2. There is power in the gift of the Holy Ghost.

The gift of the Holy Ghost is a gift of power. The Holy Ghost inspires and heals, guides and warns, enhances our natural capacities, inspires charity and humility, makes us smarter than we are, strengthens us during trials, testifies of the Father and the Son, and reveals all things to us (see 2 Nephi 32:5).

President John Taylor declared: "You may pour wealth, honor, influence, and all the luxuries of this world into the lap of man; and, destitute of the Spirit of God, he will not be happy, for that is the only source from which true happiness and comfort can come" (The Gospel Kingdom, 341).

If the Holy Ghost is the only source of true happiness, and

because the Holy Ghost will show us everything we should do, it only makes sense to learn how He communicates—or, in other words, to learn the language of revelation. After we receive the Holy Ghost, we may "speak with the tongue of angels," meaning the Lord's language, the language of revelation (2 Nephi 32:2). Our challenge is not in somehow coaxing the Lord to speak to us; our challenge is understanding what He has to say and preparing and learning how to understand Him when He speaks (see D&C 6:14).

Our challenge is not in somehow coaxing the Lord to speak to us; our challenge is understanding what He has to say and preparing and learning how to understand Him when He speaks.

I remember a time in my twenties when I was desperate for guidance on a crucial decision. I had fasted and prayed and been to the temple many times, but the answer wasn't clear. In frustration, I told a friend that I just couldn't get an answer. His simple response took me by surprise: "Have you asked the Lord to teach you *how* He communicates with you?" I hadn't, but I began that day to pray that He would.

Not long thereafter, while reading about Nephi building a ship that would carry his family across an ocean, I couldn't help but notice how clearly Nephi was able to understand specific instructions from the Lord. With that, I began to hunt for scriptural evidences of direct communication between God and man. At each one I made a little red *x* in the margin of my scriptures. Now, many years later, my scriptures are littered with little red *x*'s, each an indication that the Lord *does* communicate with His people—and often. The scriptures are the handbook for the language of revelation. They are our personal Liahona. If we will regularly immerse ourselves in the scriptures, we'll get clearer, more frequent answers to our prayers— all while learning what to do and what *not* to do to invite the presence of the Spirit.

Learning this language takes time. As a young captain charged with leading the Nephite armies, Moroni sent messengers to the prophet Alma, asking him to inquire of the Lord where the armies should go. But later in his ministry as chief captain, Moroni received inspiration for his stewardship himself. For he became "a man of a perfect understanding" (Alma 48:11)—suggesting that he learned to speak the language of revelation, perhaps even perfectly.

For the past couple of years I have been deeply troubled by a major dilemma. I have tried to do everything possible to solve the problem, to no avail. I pleaded, prayed, cried, and begged for resolution to an issue that just would not resolve itself or go away. Nothing changed, nor did I feel any closer to an answer. Then, not long ago, in the still of the night, an answer suddenly came with such clarity that I was flooded with a stream of ideas. Further, in literally a moment or two, my heart changed completely about something that had caused me great angst. Perhaps the answer, embedded in what I would call a stream of "heavenly corrective feedback," came because I was finally willing to hear what the Lord wanted me to hear. The Holy Ghost is more likely to speak to us when we're willing to listen and then act upon what we are told.

What a gift! We have access to a pure source of information, a source devoid of flattery or spin-doctoring, for "the Spirit speaketh the truth and lieth not" (Jacob 4:13). The Lord will teach us directly as much truth as we are worthy and willing to learn.

Speaking to a Churchwide audience of young adults, President Boyd K. Packer said that every Latter-day Saint "has not only the right but the obligation to understand what the gift of the Holy Ghost is." He then went on to express the regret that we too often "use it so little and so infrequently. But it is ours, and if we prepare ourselves, that voice will speak to us" (*Church News,* March 11, 2000).

The Lord will teach us directly as much truth as we are worthy and willing to learn.

Having the Holy Ghost as our constant guide and protector is essential to latter-day living and leadership. The gift of the Holy Ghost is a gift of power.

3. *There is power in the priesthood.*

By definition, priesthood power is the power and authority of God delegated to men on earth. Those who hold the priesthood have the right to say what the Lord would say if He were here. Whatever they bind on earth is bound in heaven.

Through Joseph Smith, the Aaronic Priesthood was first restored, making possible the ministering of angels and the administration of outward ordinances (see D&C 107: 20). The restoration of the Melchizedek Priesthood followed, which priesthood contains the "keys of all the spiritual blessings of the church," including the privilege of receiving the mysteries of the kingdom, having the heavens open, communing with the general assembly and church of the Firstborn, and enjoying the communion and presence of God the Father and Jesus Christ (see D&C 107:18–19).

Were it not for the restoration of priesthood power, no one could receive the gift and power of the Holy Ghost and thus have the privilege of receiving personal revelation.

Were it not for the restoration of priesthood power, no one could receive the gift and power of the Holy Ghost and thus have the privilege of receiving personal revelation; or be endowed with power in the House of the Lord (see D&C 109:22); or receive blessings of healing, comfort, strength, and instruction; or enter into the new and everlasting covenant of marriage with an eternal companion, thus launching an eternal family unit; or have a full understanding of the enabling, healing, redeeming, sanctifying power of the Atonement; or have living prophets, seers, and revelators to lead them; or bind in heaven what is bound on earth (see Matthew 16:19).

There is power in ordinances. Those who are endowed with power in the House of the Lord need never face the adversary alone. Couples worthy to be sealed at an altar in that holy house are gifted with power. The power of the priesthood heals, protects, and inoculates every righteous man and woman against the powers of darkness.

I will never forget an experience I had in Cali, Colombia. After a long evening of meetings, the presiding officer asked the congregation to remain seated while we departed. But upon the final "amen," several dozen priesthood leaders jumped to their feet and formed two lines, creating a pathway from the chapel outside to a waiting van. As we walked through this sheltered passageway, where priesthood leaders symbolized priesthood power, I was deeply moved by the metaphor. For it is the power of the priesthood that marks, clears, and protects the path leading to eternal life. Priesthood power binds heaven and earth, subdues the adversary, blesses and heals, and enables us to triumph over mortality. Every ordinance of the Melchizedek Priesthood helps prepare us to live in the presence of God. As President Harold B. Lee taught, "Through the priesthood and only the priesthood may we . . . find our way back home" (*BYU Speeches of the Year*, 1956, 2).

I am deeply grateful for the power of the priesthood and the gift of having access to this power, which when used righteously is the greatest power on earth.

4. There is power in the House of the Lord.

It is precisely because of priesthood power, the fulness of which is available only in the temple, that we may be endowed with power in the House of the Lord. The Prophet Joseph made this clear at the Kirtland Temple dedication when he prayed that the Lord's servants might "go forth from this house armed with thy power" (D&C 109:22). Simply stated, those who receive their endowment are endowed or gifted with power, and they emerge from the temple clothed in and armed with that power. From that time forward, if they keep their covenants, they are never alone, nor are they ever defenseless.

The temple is a place of refuge and revelation. I could never have handled not only the pressures and responsibilities but also the disappointments of life without regular time there. During recent years, a head-banging, hand-wringing challenge has driven me to attend even more. There have been weeks upon weeks when the only peace I felt was while in the temple. Even still, one day while I was studying the scriptures, nine words from First Nephi leaped off the page: "And I, Nephi, did go into the mount oft" (1 Nephi 18:3). Instantly I knew I needed to spend even more time in the temple, so I did—and have. The results have not been what I expected. Although I have received help with the challenge in question, as well as many others, it seems clear now that the Lord simply wanted me in the temple more where it is easier to learn certain things. That was apparently Nephi's experience as well, for as he went unto the mount oft, the Lord "showed unto [him] great things"—undoubtedly great things of the Spirit.

In the temple it becomes clear what it means to be "in but not of" the world, as we are taught that it is possible—as well as *how* it is possible—to live a higher law, even a terrestrial or celestial law, while still residing in a telestial sphere. We're taught how to draw upon the power of God. How to part the veil. How to deal with Satan. How to fulfill our foreordained missions. How to cope with suffocating pressure and heartache. And, most important, how to come into the presence of God.

The best place to learn about the temple is in the temple. Our kept covenants will eventually save us. And *that* is power!

5. *There is power in purity.*

It is possible that there is no key to accessing the power of God that is more important, more crucial than purity. While modern-day prophets have made it clear that the perfection we seek will not come in this life, they have also taught that it *is* possible to become increasingly pure—pure in our hearts, pure in our minds and motives, pure in our judgments, pure in our desires and intents, pure morally, and even pure in the way we treat and respect our physical bodies, including how we *feel* about everything from food and eating to exercise, health, piercings, tattoos, and so on. For, as the Apostle Paul taught the Corinthians, "Know ye not that your body is the temple of the Holy Ghost which is in you, which ye have of God, and ye are not your own? For ye are bought with a price: therefore glorify God in your body" (1 Corinthians 6:19–20).

How we treat our bodies—meaning, how focused we are on

> *In the temple it becomes clear what it means to be "in but not of" the world, as we are taught that it is possible—as well as how it is possible—to live a higher law, even a terrestrial or celestial law, while still residing in a telestial sphere.*

41

treating them as temples—affects our ability to receive revelation. Pure and simple, the more pure we become, the easier it is for the Holy Ghost to speak to us and work through us. As we think about purity, we may wish to consider including in our self-evaluation what we watch, read, listen to, and take into our minds. Our spirits have the remarkable capacity of being able to retain everything with which they've ever come in contact. And although in this sphere we deal with the constraints of mortality, our spirits are nonetheless receiving and cataloging everything we take into our hearts and minds.

King Benjamin warned his people: "If ye do not watch yourselves, and your thoughts, and your words, and your deeds, and observe the commandments of God, and continue in the faith of what ye have heard concerning the coming of our Lord, even unto the end of your lives, ye must perish" (Mosiah 4:30). The order of the things King Benjamin warned his people about is significant. Thoughts lead to words, (including the conversations we have with ourselves, which are often the most destructive), and words in turn lead to our actions or deeds. It is a progression that can be either productive or destructive. Hence the need to fiercely protect our minds from anything of an unholy or impure nature. No wonder the Young Women and Young Men general presidencies selected for a theme in 2007 the mandate to "let virtue garnish thy thoughts unceasingly," for the accompanying promise has a profound spiritual rippling effect: "then shall thy confidence wax strong in the presence of God" (D&C 121:45).

Confidence in the presence of God is evidence of a pure

heart. For that matter, confidence in the presence of priesthood and other leaders as well as parents is also evidence of purity.

The Prophet Joseph often spoke to the sisters of the Relief Society about keeping themselves pure. On April 28, 1842, just six days before the endowment was given for the first time, he declared that "females, if they are pure and innocent can come into the presence of God, for what is more pleasing to God than innocence. . . . If you will be pure, nothing can hinder" (Ehat and Cook, eds., *Words of Joseph Smith*, 117).

Confidence in the presence of God is evidence of a pure heart.

We may therefore wish to monitor our motives regularly in an attempt to root out selfishness and jealousy. We may need to evaluate our desires and our priorities, to review our feelings and emotions—including how we feel about people, circumstances that have developed in our lives, anyone for whom we may feel resentment, and most of all about the Lord.

The Lord has been clear about the importance of purity. In the Sermon on the Mount, He declared, "Blessed are the pure in heart: for they shall see God" (Matthew 5:8). And in this dispensation He renewed the promise in connection with temples: "And inasmuch as my people build a house unto me in the name of the Lord, and do not suffer any unclean thing to come into it, that it be not defiled, my glory shall rest upon it; . . . and my presence shall be there, for I will come into it, and all the pure in heart that shall come into it shall see God" (D&C 97:15–16).

Recently I accompanied one of my sisters and five teenage nieces to New York City. It was the first trip to the Big Apple for four of these girls, and they quickly immersed themselves in this new adventure. Prior to leaving for New York, the girls had said that they wanted to go shopping and see the sights, but that there were only two "must-have" experiences: They wanted to see a certain Broadway show, and they wanted to do baptisms in the Manhattan New York Temple—and not necessarily in that order of priority.

The first day, we tramped for hours around the city, visiting one landmark after another—from the Empire State Building to Central Park—and shopping, shopping, shopping, or at least bargain-hunting. They experienced the energy and vibrancy of New York City, and they also saw some of its filth.

Then, the next day, we experienced a stark contrast. We arose early, dressed in our Sunday best, and took a short cab ride to the Manhattan New York Temple, which is unusual in that you literally step off of a busy, dirty, New York City street into a narrow foyer, and then through beautiful doors into the temple, where a temple worker is waiting to inspect your recommend. It isn't more than three steps from the grunge of the city to the sanctity of the temple.

The difference wasn't lost on these girls. The instant we stepped inside the temple, one niece spontaneously said, "Oh, I finally feel safe." I'm not sure she had even been conscious, while walking the streets, that she had been feeling unsafe or even merely uneasy. But the contrast between the noise and jostling and stain of the world and the serenity and feeling of safety inside the temple was unmistakable. Then, to see these girls—beautiful not only because they're all adorable but even more because of their worthiness—dressed in white, performing sacred ordinances, was a striking contrast between the purity of the Lord's people and the grime of Babylon.

It *is* possible to be clean in a dirty world.

These girls carefully, selectively experienced some of the opportunities of the big city while remaining completely worthy and desirous of entering the House of the Lord. Coming unto Christ and being perfected in Him requires us to deny ourselves of all ungodliness (see Moroni 10:32).

The contrast between the noise and jostling and stain of the world and the serenity and feeling of safety inside the temple is unmistakable.

Once we set our foot on the path to godliness and purity, we can't turn back without consequences. As we steadily, within the limits of our mortal capacity, work here a little, there a little toward ever-increasing purity, what was once acceptable and appropriate to do may no longer feel or be acceptable and appropriate. We can't hit the "pause" button and say, "I want to indulge in what I used to indulge in," and go on, business as usual. It doesn't work that way. Further, when we do take a step back—and, as mortals, we'll inevitably struggle and sometimes disappoint ourselves—our vulnerabilities to the natural man increase and we're more susceptible to overindulgence and bad judgment . . . until we repent and again move forward.

If we're serious about sanctification, if we're serious about learning to draw upon the power of God, purity is key. "Sanctify yourselves," the Lord commanded the Saints of our day, adding this promise: "and ye shall be endowed with power, that ye may give even as I have spoken" (D&C 43:16).

6. *There is power in the Atonement of Jesus Christ.*

Until I was in my thirties, I thought the Atonement was basically for sinners—meaning that the Savior's grand sacrifice made it possible for us to repent. But then I suffered a heartbreaking personal loss and ensuing period of intense loneliness. During that time, and in similar times since then, I have learned that there is much more to the sublime doctrine of the Atonement. My solution initially to that devastating heartbreak many years ago was to exercise so much faith that the Lord would *have* to give me what I wanted—which was a husband and family.

Well, the Lord hasn't yet given me a husband, but He did heal my broken heart—and has done so many times since. In doing so, He taught me that He not only paid the price for sin but compensated for all of the pain we experience in this life. Because of His Atonement, we have access to His grace, or *enabling* power, and to His *redemptive* power—power that frees us from sin; power to be healed emotionally, physically, and spiritually; power to mend our broken hearts and to free us from all manner of captivity (Luke 4:18); power to loose the bands of death (Alma 7:12); power to do good works; power to turn weakness into strength (Ether 12:27); and power to receive salvation through faith on His name. It is because of the Atonement that, if we build our foundation on Christ, the devil can have no power over us (see Helaman 5:12). It is because of the power and reach of the Atonement that we can triumph over death itself and rise again.

There is power in God the Father and His Son Jesus Christ—power that, because of the Atonement of Jesus Christ, we may access through the word of God, the Holy Ghost, the priesthood, increasing personal purity, and the ordinances of the holy temple.

*The truths of the gospel are not meant to discourage in any
way. Though doctrines inevitably stretch us, perhaps they also
bring a feeling of reassurance that if we will learn to draw upon the
power of God, we will not shrink. We will go forward, unflinching, unswerving, indomitable, making the world safer and cleaner,
until we've done everything we were born to do.*

CHAPTER THREE

DRAWING UPON THE POWERS OF HEAVEN

We are wanderers in a strange land, pilgrims on a pilgrimage to return to our Father's presence. We are sons and daughters removed for a season from the direct presence of our Father and the heavenly host with whom we became so familiar and by whom we were likely taught during our premortality.

President Joseph Fielding Smith explained why we have such a desire to return to the presence of the Father: "There is not a soul in this room, not one, that has not seen him. You do not remember it, I do not remember it, but nevertheless there was a time before we ever came into this world when we dwelt in his presence. We knew what kind of a being he is. One thing we saw was how glorious he is. Another thing, how great was his wisdom, his understanding, how wonderful was his power and his inspiration. And we wanted to be like him. And because we wanted to be like him, we are here. . . . We saw him in his glory and it was made known to us that by keeping his commandments and observing every covenant that would be given to us on this earth, we could come back again into his presence" (*Take Heed to Yourselves!* 345).

Although our period of probation requires us to endure and triumph (with God's help) over a telestial environment, in the Father's grand mercy, He has not required us to brave this experience alone—meaning, without Him. Mortality may be a test, but it is an open-book test.

What then must we do to qualify for and learn to access His power?

Consider some of the following:

First, *it all begins with faith—our faith.* Faith is the first principle of the gospel because faith is a principle of action and power that influences, at least to some degree, the Lord's intervention in our lives.

Faith is the first principle of the gospel because faith is a principle of action and power that influences, at least to some degree, the Lord's intervention in our lives.

By faith Enoch and his people were translated, even such that they did not see death. Abraham was prepared to offer his beloved son as a sacrifice, when commanded to do so, "accounting that God was able to raise him up, even from the dead" (Hebrews 11:19). Sarah gave birth "when she was past age," and she did so—and here is the crucial qualifier—"because *she judged him faithful* who had promised" (Hebrews 11:11;

50

emphasis added). Nephi subdued Laban, not to mention his elder brothers; Captain Moroni led the Nephite armies to victory because "he was a man who was firm in the faith of Christ" (Alma 48:13); and the sons of Helaman were miraculously preserved in the midst of battle because their mothers had taught them that "if they did not doubt, God would deliver them" (Alma 56:47). So great was the faith of the fourteen-year-old Joseph Smith that when he went into a grove of trees and asked "in faith, nothing wavering" (James 1:6), the Father and the Son appeared, ushering in the Restoration.

The righteous of all ages have demonstrated again and again that "without faith it is impossible to please [God]: for he that cometh to God must believe that he is, and that he is a rewarder of them that diligently seek him" (Hebrews 11:6). Simply stated, our Father rewards them who believe in His Son. Elder James E. Talmage taught that "faith is of itself a principle of power; and by its presence or absence, by its fulness or paucity, even the Lord was and is influenced, and in great measure controlled, in the bestowal or withholding of blessings; for He ministers according to law, and not with caprice or uncertainty" (Jesus the Christ, 296).

Soon after President Gordon B. Hinckley was called to serve as a counselor to President Spencer W. Kimball, in July 1981, the health of the prophet and his two other counselors failed, leaving President Hinckley to shoulder the burden of the First Presidency largely alone. At one point he recorded: "The responsibility I carry frightens me. . . . Sometimes I could weep with concern. But there comes the assurance that the Lord put me here for His purpose, and if I will be humble and seek the direction of the Holy Spirit, He will use me . . . to accomplish His purposes" (Dew, *Go Forward with Faith*, 393).

Throughout his life, President Hinckley's practice has been simply to go forward with faith, including during his most advanced years, when he has found it necessary to go forward alone, without his companion at his side, and during which time he has faced the most serious illness of his life. And yet he has pushed forward.

Challenges that tax our faith are usually opportunities to stretch and strengthen our faith by finding out if we really believe the Lord will help us.

Challenges that tax our faith are usually opportunities to stretch and strengthen our faith by finding out if we really believe the Lord will help us.

If your faith is wobbly, if you're not sure the Lord will come to your aid, experiment. Put Him to the test. A great place to start is in the scriptures, for as Jacob wrote: "We search the prophets, and we have many revelations . . . and having all these witnesses we obtain a hope, and our faith becometh unshaken" (Jacob 4:6).

Unshaken faith activates the power of God in our lives, "for he worketh by power, according to the faith of the children of men" (Moroni 10:7).

Second, it is incumbent upon us to repent. Faith in Jesus Christ leads us to repent, or turn away from, sins that hold us spiritually captive, and to obey with exactness. Great power follows those who repent and obey.

Lamoni's father pledged to "give away" all his sins to know God (Alma 22:18). Undoubtedly, every one of us has sins he or she needs to give away. An important question, then, is: What favorite sins, large or small, are you willing to give away—right now, today—in order to increase your access to the power of God? Again, if we're serious about sanctification, repentance is not optional.

In contrast to sin, which is ugly and costly, obedience is brilliant and its fruits are endless. One of those fruits is happiness. *The only way to be happy is to live the gospel.*

It is not possible to sin enough to be happy. It isn't possible to buy enough to be happy, or to entertain or indulge or pamper ourselves enough to be happy. It is not possible to hide enough or run far enough away from trials and troubles to be happy. Happiness and joy come only when we are living up to who we are. King Benjamin understood this and taught it clearly when he admonished us to "consider on the blessed and happy state of those that keep the commandments of God. For . . . they are blessed in all things, . . . and if they hold out faithful to the end . . . they may dwell with God in a state of never-ending happiness" (Mosiah 2:41).

Satan likely bristles at this principle, for happiness is something the ultimate narcissist will never experience. I have never met anyone who was happier because he was immoral, or because he was addicted to something, or because he was dishonest and compromised his integrity. The Lord has blessed us with covenants that keep us on the straight and narrow path because this "road less traveled" is actually the easier road. It is so much easier to be righteous than to sin, so much easier to deal with a clear conscience than one ravaged by guilt, so much easier to feel peace of mind and heart when we are living up to who we are rather than coping with the emotional and spiritual ravages of regret, knowing we have lived beneath our divine nature.

The happiest people I know are those who repent regularly and obey. And a major reason for their happiness is that they have increased confidence in approaching and petitioning the Lord and increased access to His power.

The happiest people I know are those who repent regularly and obey.

The third thing we can do to increase the power of God in our lives is to diligently seek. There is perhaps no more frequent invitation or reassuring promise in all of scripture than this one: "Seek me diligently and ye shall find me; ask, and ye shall receive; knock, and it shall be opened unto you" (D&C 88:63).

Notice that God never said, "Seek me a zillion times. Beg again and again. And maybe, just maybe, if you're lucky, if you jump through enough hoops enough times, and if I feel like it, I'll help you a little." To the contrary, the two greatest of all Beings are ever ready to help us. No call waiting. No voice mail. No capriciousness or uncertainty or whimsy. Theirs is the most instant of instant messaging. In the words of John, "This is the confidence that we have in him, that, if we ask any thing according to his will, he heareth us" (1 John 5:14). President Spencer W. Kimball declared this about our Father and His Son's willingness to speak to us: "Someone has said that we live in a day in which God, if there be a God, chooses to be silent, but The Church of Jesus Christ of Latter-day Saints proclaims to the world that neither the Father nor the Son is silent. They are vocal and . . . constantly express a willingness, indeed an eagerness, to maintain communication with men" (*Faith Precedes the Miracle*, 65–66).

Nonetheless, and in spite of this eagerness, neither the Father nor His Son will force anything upon us. Though They want to help us, and have offered to share everything with us, how much knowledge and power we obtain is entirely up to us.

Most of the revelations received by the Prophet Joseph came after diligent seeking, including this magnificent promise: "I, the Lord, . . . delight to honor those who serve me in righteousness. . . . Great shall be their reward and eternal shall be their glory. And to them will I reveal all mysteries. . . . And their wisdom shall be great, and their understanding reach to heaven. . . . For . . . by my power will I make known unto them the secrets of my will" (D&C 76:5–10). The Lord seems to have set no limits on what He is willing to teach us and give us. We are the only ones who set limits—through our neglect or disobedience or ignorance.

We are in large measure the ones who determine what we will learn and experience in mortality, and what we will receive eternally.

The question, then, is this: How much power do we want to have, and what are we willing to do to obtain it? Heber C. Kimball said that "the greatest torment [the Prophet Joseph] had . . . was because this people would not live up to their [spiritual] privileges. . . . He said sometimes that he felt pressed upon as though he were pent up in an acorn shell, and all because the people did not and would not prepare themselves to receive the rich treasures of wisdom and knowledge that he had to impart. He could have revealed a great many things to us if we had been ready" (in *Journal of Discourses*, 10:167).

How much power do we want to have, and what are we willing to do to obtain it?

Spiritual privileges that call forth the powers of heaven are available to *all* who diligently seek them. *Will we diligently seek?* Consider this classic passage from Alma: "*Whosoever will come* may come and partake of the waters of life freely; and whosoever will not come the same is not compelled to come" (Alma 42:27; emphasis added). Notice it doesn't say that just the popular ones or the smart ones or the ones who have nine children who all served missions may come. It says *whosoever will*—meaning, it is our choice.

Those who serve missions don't ask investigators, Would you *like* to come to Church? Would you like to be baptized? They ask, *Will you* come? *Will you* be baptized?

So may I ask, *Will you* increase your faith? *Will you* repent and obey? *Will you* diligently seek? *Will you* learn to access the power of God so that you can live up to the heavenly recommendations that placed you here now, so that you can help destroy the "beautiful wickedness" that abounds? *Will you* do what you were born to do?

In his last major address as Prime Minister, and while World War II still raged in the Pacific, Winston Churchill said to his countrymen: "I told you hard things at the beginning of [this war]; you did not shrink, and I should be unworthy of your confidence . . . if I did not still cry; Forward, unflinching, unswerving, indomitable, till the whole task is done and the whole world is safe and clean" (Cannadine, *Speeches of Winston Churchill*, 266).

There is really only one way to go forward, unflinching, unswerving, and indomitable, until all of the work of this dispensation is done and the whole world is safe and clean, and that is by learning to hear the voice of the Spirit, by learning how to draw upon the power of the Father and His Son.

President Spencer W. Kimball reassured us that doing so is imminently possible: "The Almighty is with this people. We shall have all the revelations that we shall need if we will do our duty and keep the commandments of God. . . . If there be eyes to see, there will be visions to inspire. If there be ears to hear, there will be revelations to experience. If there be hearts which can understand, know this: that the exalting truths of Christ's gospel will no longer be hidden and mysterious, and all earnest seekers may know God and his program" (in *Conference Report*, October 1966, 26).

You may feel that some of the pages to follow share hard

things. The truths of the gospel are not meant to discourage in any way. Though doctrines inevitably stretch us, perhaps they also bring a feeling of reassurance that if we will learn to draw upon the power of God, we will not shrink. We will go forward, unflinching, unswerving, indomitable, making the world safer and cleaner, until we've done everything we were born to do. *For we were born to lead. We were born to build Zion. We were born for glory.* Everything we do in life should be measured against this grand standard.

President Gordon B. Hinckley said it this way: "You can be a leader. You *must* be a leader . . . in those causes for which the Church stands. . . . The adversary of all truth would put into your heart a reluctance to make an effort. Cast that fear aside and be valiant in the cause of truth and righteousness" (*Church News*, September 21, 1996, 3; emphasis added).

Thus, in the words of Moroni, may we seek this Jesus of whom the apostles and prophets have written (see Ether 12:41) so that we can experience for ourselves the power in Jesus Christ to strengthen us, to sanctify us, to help us run this leg of the relay. Don't ever underestimate the power of Jesus Christ to help us. Isaiah said it this way: "Hast thou not known? hast thou not heard, that the everlasting God . . . the Creator of the ends of the earth . . . giveth power to the faint; and to them that have no might he increaseth strength. . . . They that wait upon the Lord shall renew their

Don't ever underestimate the power of Jesus Christ to help us.

strength; they shall mount up with wings as eagles; they shall run, and not be weary; and they shall walk, and not faint" (Isaiah 40:28–31).

I have learned for myself that this is true. Because of our Father and His Son, we don't have to run our leg of the relay alone. We have access to the greatest and grandest of all power. And when we have the power of God with us, we truly can do all things.

When things aren't going well, when you want to quit, when it seems as though nothing is working, and certainly when your forward progress stops, the solution is often simply to back up.

CHAPTER FOUR

GOING FORWARD BY BACKING UP

W e tend to think of *repentance* as penitence, sorrow for and turning from sin, which of course it is. But another definition of the word *repent* is "to change." Taking both definitions into consideration, it is interesting to consider the reasons Alma may have counseled his people at the waters of Mormon to preach nothing to the people save faith in the Lord and repentance (see Mosiah 18:20). Learning to change—and being willing to change—are crucial virtues in our eternal progression. And changing usually involves backing up.

During last year's holiday season, a good news/bad news situation developed for the company for which I work. The good news was that we were inundated with orders—from bookstores, chain stores, customers . . . everyone, it seemed, with the volume of orders being considerably larger than ever before. The bad news? The sophisticated fulfillment system in our distribution center on the west side of the Salt Lake Valley was overwhelmed. And in early December it became clear that we had to do something drastic or risk disappointing many customers. The only solution was to "break" the automated system running the warehouse by disabling certain functions so we could fill the orders manually.

But that meant we needed many more workers to staff round-the-clock shifts running six days a week. At the time, Utah had one of the lowest unemployment rates in the country, and there were not enough workers to be found. So we "invited" our corporate-office employees working in downtown Salt Lake City to each work a few swing or graveyard shifts at the warehouse. That meant all of us (and I pause here to say that our employees were champs and proved willing to do whatever was needed), so for several nights running during the month of December, I worked graveyards at the warehouse alongside many of my corporate-office colleagues.

One night, or early morning, around 1:00 A.M., there was a lull in my particular assembly-line job, so I decided to run to a nearby all-night grocery store to buy treats for everyone who was working the night shift. I told a couple of my colleagues where I was going, that I'd be back in half an hour, and dashed out the door. Moments later I was zipping unobstructed along a thoroughfare on the west side of the Salt Lake Valley when suddenly, *BAM!* I hit something, and hit it hard. My adrenaline began pumping out of control as the horrifying thought that I had hit *someone* flashed across my mind. At the same time, the car began to vibrate and veer sharply to the right, and it was all I could do to steer the vehicle to the side of the road before it came to a dead stop.

I hunted unsuccessfully for a flashlight, got out of the car and down on my hands and knees, and peered under the engine compartment. It seemed unusually dark, and all I could see was something big and black wedged between the road and the undercarriage. I couldn't tell if the big black thing was what I'd hit and dragged along, or if somehow I'd dislodged the engine itself and it had fallen to the ground. At the moment, that seemed irrelevant anyway, because the car would not budge regardless. I got back in the driver's seat, offered a prayer, found a number for roadside assistance, and reached an operator. Explaining that my vehicle was completely disabled, I told him I needed a wrecker, and pronto, because I was in a warehouse district at 1:30 in the morning—alone. To make matters a little more interesting, off in the distance, about a block away, I could see what looked like a group of men heading my way.

The operator seemed but marginally interested in my plight, and I was on hold for what seemed like the duration of *Gone with the Wind*. Finally he came back with the news that he'd located a wrecker but that it would be two hours before he could get there. "Oh, no!" I blurted. "In two hours, I'll be dead . . . or at least maimed. Please, you've got to find someone who can come sooner." Again he put me on hold, until finally I hung up, offered another prayer, and was about to call 911 when a police car with red rotating lights pulled up behind me. I can't remember ever having been happy to see those rotating red lights before—particularly *behind* me—but that night I was ecstatic, and I breathed for the first time in an hour.

A kind officer quickly assessed the situation, pulled out his flashlight, and peered underneath the car. It was as he was saying that he couldn't tell either exactly what had happened, when a thought suddenly occurred to me—a thought that certainly would have saved a lot of time and grief if it had come one hour earlier. Nonetheless, I said to the officer, "I wonder if I should try backing up. The car won't go forward, not even an inch, but if that black thing is what I hit, maybe backing up would dislodge it." He agreed it was worth a try, so I got in the car, put it in reverse, and backed up a few inches, at which point an ugly, black, metal object popped out. "Oh my goodness," the officer said, holding up the heavy, misshapen object, "do you know what this is?" I shook my head no. I'd never seen anything like what he was holding. "It's a street lamp," he said. "No wonder it's so dark on this stretch of road." He pointed up at the top of a nearby lamppost that was conspicuously absent a street lamp.

We checked underneath the car to make sure nothing had been punctured, I thanked him for his help, and a few moments later, I was back in my car once again zipping down the road as though nothing had happened.

There are three lessons from the Parable of the Street Lamp. First, when there's no light, it's dark. For "that which doth not edify is not of God, and is darkness." On the other hand, "that which is of God is light; and he that receiveth light, and continueth in God, receiveth more light; and that light groweth brighter and brighter until the perfect day" (D&C 50:23–24). To what end? "That you may chase darkness from among you" (D&C 50:25). Jesus Christ is the source of all light. When He's not present, it's dark, hard to see, and we're much more likely to hit big, ugly objects along the way.

Jesus Christ is the source of all light. When He's not present, it's dark.

Second, even though that metal street lamp was heavy (about forty pounds) and big (two feet in diameter), compared to the size of my SUV, it was small. And yet that relatively small object completely disabled my vehicle and stopped my forward progress. The message? When our forward progress stops, particularly our forward spiritual progress, it almost always starts with something relatively small. We refuse to apologize, or to accept an apology. We stop praying or become lax in our personal worship and study. We tell a little lie, which we later have to cover with a bigger lie, and on it goes. We promise to do something we never intended to do, or couldn't resist passing along a story about a friend, or decided that when our bishop didn't handle something particularly well we'd choose to be offended, and on and on.

When our forward-moving spiritual progress stops, that process almost always begins with something small. An oft-repeated but instructive episode from Church history is that of Thomas B. Marsh, then president of the Quorum of the Twelve, and his wife, who argued with Sister Harris over cream obtained from the same cow. Their bickering and dispute over a minor incident led eventually to the Marshes' excommunication and their separation from the Church for nearly twenty years.

Said Elder Neal A. Maxwell: "When people fall, they *do not suddenly stop believing* in the atonement; they simply start believing in their impulses. Their discipline disappears as their perspective shrinks. Irrationality replaces illumination" (*We Will Prove Them Herewith*, 26; emphasis added).

Again, when our forward spiritual progress stops, that process so very often begins with something small, even inestimably minute, which if corrected or repented of quickly would end the matter. But unrepented sin, even *small* unrepented sin, gives Lucifer an opening that he subsequently does everything within his considerable power to exploit. Like the proverbial camel with his nose in the nomad's tent, Satan needs only a small opening to infiltrate an entire life. Thus the reason to repent *quickly* and move on. This is the second lesson of the Parable of the Street Lamp.

Unrepented sin, even small unrepented sin, gives Lucifer an opening that he subsequently does everything within his considerable power to exploit.

The third lesson is that when things aren't going well, when you want to quit, when it seems as though nothing is working, and certainly when your forward progress stops, the solution is often simply to back up.

Backing up may mean repenting. It may mean forgiving someone or seeking forgiveness of another. It may just mean trying again. It may require you to ask for help, seek knowledge, humble yourself, change a decision, change an attitude, change your heart, or mend a relationship. It may mean striving harder to become more pure. It may mean that it's time to stop doing something or start doing something. It may mean seeking counsel from a parent or a priesthood leader, a trusted friend or even a professional. Whatever backing up means—and it can mean something different for every unique situation—there are many times in life when we simply need to back up, even just a few inches, before we can hope to zoom forward spiritually again. In fact, life is in many respects a continuous exercise in stopping, backing up, making changes, and then going forward.

> *Whatever backing up means—and it can mean something different for every unique situation— there are many times in life when we simply need to back up, even just a few inches, before we can hope to zoom forward spiritually again.*

The scriptures are replete with examples of this pattern. The story of Amulek is classic. A prominent citizen of Ammonihah, Amulek saw his whole life change when an angel appeared to him and instructed him to return home and there "receive" a prophet of the Lord. By the world's standards, Amulek wouldn't have been a candidate for such an honor, but the Lord knew differently.

Amulek had become caught up in the ways and workings of the world. He was, in his own words, a "man of no small reputation" who had "many kindreds and friends," and who had "acquired much riches by the hand of [his] industry" (Alma 10:4). He chose to describe himself entirely in worldly terms— he was famous, rich, and had lots of friends.

Then his autobiographical account continues with an interesting twist. "I never have known much of the ways of the Lord, and his mysteries and marvelous power," he acknowledges. Then, in an uncharacteristic moment of reflection and humility, Amulek stops and backs up. One can almost imagine him saying, "Oops!" For he reversed or at least corrected himself with the next statement: "I said I never had known much of these things; but behold, I mistake, for I have seen much of his mysteries and his marvelous power. . . . Nevertheless, I did harden my heart, for I was called many times and I would not hear; therefore I knew concerning these things, yet I would not know; therefore I went on rebelling against God" (Alma 10:5–6).

The story of Amulek is a story for our day. It is the story of someone who became consumed with the world, but then, to his everlasting credit, backed up. Backing up in his case meant acknowledging the error of his ways. It probably required repentance. It certainly entailed changing his focus, outlook, and attitude, and it required him to turn around and head another direction. The combination of backing up and turning around resulted in a profound spiritual awakening that ultimately changed both his life here and the course of his eternal life. For from that time, he went forward with the prophet Alma, preaching repentance and testifying and prophesying of Jesus Christ.

One verse summarizes what happened to Amulek because he backed up and turned around: "And Alma and Amulek came forth out of the prison, and they were not hurt; for the Lord had granted unto them power, according to their faith which was in Christ. And they straightway came forth out of the prison; and they were loosed from their bands; and the prison had fallen to the earth, and every soul within the walls thereof, save it were Alma and Amulek, was slain" (Alma 14:28). Because Amulek backed up, repented, changed, turned around, and went forth in the strength of the Lord, he learned how to call upon the power of Jesus Christ to such a degree that when prison walls came tumbling down around him and Alma, to the destruction of everyone else, they survived.

There are numerous other scriptural protagonists who modeled the virtues of backing up and turning around. Alma was a priest in the court of the wicked King Noah, on a path to almost certain spiritual destruction, when he heard Abinadi testify of Christ and believed his words. Alma repented of his transgressions, was forced to flee for his life, and at great personal risk taught believers who gathered at the waters of Mormon. His ministry began when, upon hearing the truth, he backed up, acknowledged and repented of his sins, turned around, and went forward a new man, with a new heart.

Alma the Younger and the sons of Mosiah changed from paths of rebellion, apostasy, and idolatry to lives of extraordinary missionary service. Saul made sport of persecuting Christians until the Lord appeared to him and called him to repentance. And "straightway" he went forward preaching and testifying of Christ (see Acts 9:20). While hunting in a secluded forest, Enos pled with the Lord in mighty prayer, received the personal revelation that his sins were forgiven and that he would be blessed, and went forward preaching and prophesying. After a series of remarkable experiences communicating with the Lord, the brother of Jared became lax in his personal devotions—until, that is, "the Lord came again unto the brother of Jared, and stood in a cloud and talked with him. And for the space of three hours did the Lord talk with the brother of Jared, and chastened him because he remembered not to call upon the name of the Lord." Three hours of chastening by the Lord Himself had its effect: "And the brother of Jared repented of the evil which he had done, and did call upon the name of the Lord" (Ether 2:14–15).

In each of these instances, these men repented, and the Lord in turn changed their hearts, bringing them out of a "deep sleep" as they "awoke unto God," had a mighty change wrought in their hearts, and received His image in their countenances (see Alma 5:7, 12–14). This is backing up and turning around of the highest magnitude. It is what President Spencer W. Kimball referred to when he declared, "There is no royal road to repentance: whether he be a president's son or a king's daughter, an emperor's prince or a lowly peasant, he must himself repent and his repentance must be personal and individual and humble" (*Teachings of Spener W. Kimball*, 86–87).

Sometimes backing up and turning around involves submitting yourself to the Lord's will, and thus being willing to do something you never would have chosen.

Moroni thought his life was at an end. His father, Mormon, was gone. Every Nephite who would not deny the Christ was being put to death. But Moroni would not deny the Christ, so, in vagabond-like fashion, he wandered wherever he could find safety. He supposed he'd done all the writing he was going to do, but then wrote this: "I had supposed not to have written any more; but I write a few more things, that perhaps they may be of worth unto my brethren, the Lamanites, in some future day" (Moroni 1:4). Homeless, alone, and no doubt lonely, Moroni nonetheless went on to record some of the great discourses in the Book of Mormon, including the quintessential sermon on faith, hope, and charity. For Moroni, backing up represented a change of heart and even a change of plans. And all who read that sacred book are the benefactors of his goodness, his persistence, and his obedience.

> *Sometimes backing up and turning around involves submitting yourself to the Lord's will, and thus being willing to do something you never would have chosen.*

After the wicked Laban stole the gold and other riches Nephi and his brothers offered him in exchange for the brass plates, and then tried to slay the four brothers, Laman and Lemuel murmured, beat Nephi and Sam with a rod, and initially refused to make another attempt to get the plates. Rather than be dissuaded by his older brothers, Nephi backed up by refusing to give up, trying again to persuade his brothers to go again to Laban's house, and finally succeeding.

Later, when the Spirit constrained him to kill Laban, Nephi backed up again. "I shrunk and would that I might not slay him," he recorded. But when the Spirit repeated the instruction to slay Laban, explaining that "the Lord slayeth the wicked to bring forth his righteous purposes," for "it is better that one man should perish than that a nation should dwindle and perish in unbelief," Nephi changed his position and did as instructed (see 1 Nephi 4:6–8). Nephi demonstrated his willingness to back up by being obedient to spiritual promptings that, in the moment, were difficult to accept or understand.

Life is all about backing up, because, ironically, backing up in its various forms is what ensures progression. We of all people believe in eternal progression. We teach and preach of it constantly, and perhaps in the repetition sometimes imagine it to be something that we'll care about in the great beyond but that isn't really relevant to us right here, right now.

Yet, our eternal progression is taking place right now, today. We believe that we are sons and daughters of God, and that we have the potential not only to return to live with Him but to actually become as He is. This perhaps goes without saying, but the only way to get from where we are, wherever that is, to where God is, is to progress—persistently, regularly, and eternally.

Inherent within the concept of progression is the fact that some days we do better than others. We all make mistakes. Most of us make them regularly. Our Father expected this, for He is now an exalted, glorious Being who knows all, understands all, and foresees all. That is why He gave us His Son, so that we could repent and be forgiven, be healed from our mistakes, be strengthened, and then move on.

But He understood completely that we would have ups and downs. We try to change, start over, make progress in one area and sometimes slip back in others. Some days we live beneath ourselves and need to back up and even turn around, while on other days we zoom forward with confidence and determination, the Spirit as our guide. Some days our faith is strong; other days it can be a little wobbly. We handle some challenges well, while letting others stall our progress or even get the best of us. But through it all, if we "press forward with a steadfastness in Christ," feasting upon His word and enduring to the end, we will have eternal life (see 2 Nephi 31:20). Thus, the very nature of progression suggests we are slowly but steadily moving upward and onward, learning and growing, backing up and turning around, going on to gain more knowledge and experience, elevating our habits, purifying our hearts and motives, and gradually becoming the men and women we are destined to be.

A friend of mine serving with her husband as he presides over a mission signs her letters *O&U*—Onward and Upward. I love the image and the expression. This life is not about perfection, but progression. It's about persistently, consciously pressing forward—*Onward*—and persistently, consciously trying to elevate everything from our habits to our pursuits—*Upward*. The irony is that in order to continue Onward and Upward, we often have to back up and change something about our attitude, our approach, our habits, our mistakes, our understanding.

> *This life is not about perfection, but progression. It's about persistently, consciously pressing forward.*

The Prophet Joseph Smith taught that "our Master is absent only for a little season, and at the end of it He will call each to render an account; and where the five talents were bestowed, ten will be required; and he that has made no improvement will be cast out as an unprofitable servant" (*Teachings*, 68). On another occasion he said, "I advise all to go on to perfection, and search deeper and deeper into the mysteries of Godliness" (*Teachings*, 364).

The course we seek is to be steady and constant, regularly making course corrections and improvement, backing up and turning around as necessary, but always generally moving forward. Onward and Upward. Such are the characteristics of latter-day men and women of God who know that Jesus is the Christ and that His gospel has been restored, who have committed to follow Him, who through regular backing up become increasingly pure, and who therefore increasingly qualify to call upon His power.

*The only way to fight the fire and brimstone of hell prepared
for Lucifer and those who follow him is through the fire of faith in
the Lord Jesus Christ, the fire of testimony in His divinity, and the
baptism of fire and of the Holy Ghost.*

CHAPTER FIVE

YOU *CAN* FIGHT FIRE WITH FIRE

I wish I had a dollar for every time I've heard someone say, usually tongue-in-cheek and typically in response to another person's fascination with bank accounts or RVs or designer homes or stock portfolios or things with engines that go vroom vroom, "You can't take it with you." Meaning, of course, that it would be pointless—even wasteful—to line one's coffin with gold coins or jewelry or awards, because such earthly treasures would do nothing more than rust and eventually rot. When it is our time to step across the veil, our mortality and probation completed, we leave almost everything behind. *Almost* everything. Hold that thought.

Another phrase that has worked its way into our cultural vernacular—"You can't fight fire with fire"—is actually a misconception. As it turns out, you *can* fight fire with fire. Firefighters frequently use controlled burns in national forests and preserves to help native plants regenerate in their respective ecosystems and prevent out-of-control forest fires. It is a technique firefighters have embraced only in recent decades, but one utilized by First Nations tribes for centuries to control their surroundings and enable their environment to regenerate.

In short, there are some things—in fact, *everything* that's important—you can take with you. Happily, death does not bring an end to *anything* important—covenants, eternal families, friendships and socialities, personal purity, knowledge, and our testimonies of the Risen Lord and His gospel. And it is possible—in fact, imperative—that we fight fire with fire.

> *Happily, death does not bring an end to anything important—covenants, eternal families, friendships and socialities, personal purity, knowledge, and our testimonies of the Risen Lord and His gospel.*

Fire is spoken of and used in diverse ways by the Lord and throughout holy writ. Consider the subheadings that appear under "Fire" in the *Topical Guide:* "Earth, Cleansing of; Flame; God, Presence of; God, Spirit of; Hell; Holy Ghost, Baptism of; Transfiguration; World, End of." Fire is used to typify the glory and power of God, sanctification, and even the Lord Jehovah Himself on the one hand, and hell and damnation on the other.

An angel of the Lord appeared unto Moses "in a flame of fire out of the midst of a bush: and he looked, and, behold, the bush burned with fire, and the bush was not consumed" (Exodus 3:2). During the Savior's ministry to the Nephites on the Temple Mount at Bountiful, the people "saw angels descending out of heaven as it were in the midst of fire; and they came down and encircled those little ones about, and they were encircled about with fire; and the angels did minister unto them" (3 Nephi 17:24). Later, when Nephi baptized the Twelve the Savior had chosen as His disciples, they were "filled with the Holy Ghost and with fire. And behold, they were encircled about as if it were by fire," after which first angels and then the Savior ministered unto them (3 Nephi 19:13–15). Shadrach, Meshach, and Abed-nego were cast into a "burning fiery furnace" (Daniel 3:20) when they refused King Nebuchadnezzar's command to do something that would violate their covenants, but they emerged completely unscathed.

The Prophet Joseph Smith taught that God dwells in eternal fire, meaning glory (see *Teachings*, 326, 367). He saw in vision "the transcendent beauty of the gate through which the heirs of [the celestial] kingdom will enter, which was like unto circling flames of fire; also the blazing throne of God, whereon was seated the Father and the Son" (D&C 137:2–3). Repeatedly, *fire* is used to depict holiness and the Lord.

On the other hand, fire is also used frequently to depict Lucifer and the realm of damnation. The Lord "rained upon Sodom and Gomorrah brimstone and fire from the Lord out of heaven" (Genesis 19:24). In the parable of the wheat and the tares, the Savior taught that at the end of the world the tares would be gathered and burned in the fire (see Matthew

13:24–30), for ultimately this world will be cleansed and "burned with fire" (Jacob 6:3). Further, the Lord has promised that "the righteous shall be gathered on my right hand unto eternal life; and the wicked on my left hand will I be ashamed to own before the Father; Wherefore I will say unto them—Depart from me, ye cursed, into everlasting fire, prepared for the devil and his angels" (D&C 29:27–28). Those who ultimately stand ashamed and guilty before the bar of God will be sentenced to that "lake of fire and brimstone, whose flames are unquenchable, and whose smoke ascendeth up forever and ever, which lake of fire and brimstone is endless torment" (Jacob 6:10).

Interestingly and ironically, it seems clear that the only way to fight the fire and brimstone of hell prepared for Lucifer and those who follow him is through the fire of faith in the Lord Jesus Christ, the fire of testimony in His divinity, and the "baptism of fire and of the Holy Ghost" (2 Nephi 31:14). Indeed, this baptism of fire and the Holy Ghost, or the Comforter, "showeth all things, and teacheth the peaceable things of the kingdom" (D&C 39:6).

The fire of faith in the Lord Jesus Christ, the fire of testimony of His divinity—that He is our Savior, the Son of God, Redeemer of all who choose to repent, cast aside their nets, and follow Him—the baptism of fire and the Holy Ghost is the only sure way to fight and fend off the threat of "everlasting burning" (Mosiah 27:28). And we can and will take our faith and testimony with us.

An experience of a year ago caused me to think about this in a new way. One Sunday afternoon I became suddenly, horribly, and inexplicably ill with sharp, hideous pain. I later learned I was dealing with kidney stones, and wow, THEY HURT! Because I had never experienced anything of that nature, my physician ordered a battery of tests. One test led to another, and the long story made short is that I was diagnosed with cancer—the same kind of cancer my mother was diagnosed with at my age.

Hearing the dreaded "C word" is traumatizing! And at first almost paralyzing. In my case, the news was complicated by the fact that I had watched my mother endure major surgery, followed by a year's worth of hideous chemotherapy during which the chemo triggered a blood clot in her lung. It was a rigorous, painful, agonizing period. Her cancer had spread far enough that for several years we dealt with the anxiety of wondering if the treatment had worked. Happily, our mother is still alive, but when I heard my own diagnosis, the memory of that difficult time consumed me. The thought of having to go through what she'd gone through panicked me.

As it turned out, though, my situation proved to be completely different from my mother's. Though our diagnoses were the same, there was one major difference: Thanks to the kidney stone, which had triggered all of those tests, we caught my cancer early. *Very* early. I too had to have surgery, but mine was a simple, outpatient procedure that required just a couple of days' recovery. And the prescribed follow-up treatment has been regular checkups. No radiation. No chemotherapy. Just trips every six months to the specialist for follow-up tests. The difference between my cancer and my mother's was early detection. A gifted radiologist caught mine as early as it could have been detected. As a result, I avoided major surgery, major treatment, and years of anxiety.

There is good reason to do things early. As one small example, the leaders of the Church always arrive at meetings early and are on the stand in plenty of time to thoughtfully prepare for the meeting about to begin. You won't see them slipping into general conference at the last moment. Even the First Presidency, who enter after other General Authorities and general officers, arrive in plenty of time to spend a few minutes quietly and respectfully pondering what is about to take place and preparing their hearts for worship.

The Lord has something to say about doing things early, particularly as it relates to Him: "He that seeketh me early shall find me" (D&C 88:83).

The Lord has something to say about doing things early, particularly as it relates to Him: "He that seeketh me early shall find me" (D&C 88:83). That injunction could mean many things: early in the morning, early in the day, early in a relationship, early in a marriage, early in a family, early when trouble strikes or when we sin or make a mistake, early when we're discouraged or disappointed or sad, early when we feel loneliness settling in, early when we're not quite sure how to teach a child or handle a complicated situation. Early.

The invitation to seek the Lord early also suggests seeking Him first. Turning to Him before anyone or anything else.

Listening to Him and His called servants before considering the counsel of anyone else. Following Him first. Seeking after Him and His ways rather than the ways of the world.

Disciples of Jesus Christ put Him first. And in doing so, they become empowered to fight the fire of Lucifer's constant enticements that lead only to damnation. They carry within them the fire of faith in Jesus Christ.

Elder Henry B. Eyring taught it this way: "Most of us have thought about how to prepare for storms. We have seen and felt the suffering of women, men, and children . . . caught in hurricanes, tsunamis, wars, and droughts. One reaction is to ask, 'How can I be prepared?' And there is a rush to buy and put away whatever people think they might need for the day they might face such calamities. But there is another even more important preparation we must make for tests that are certain to come to each of us. That preparation must be started far in advance because it takes time. What we will need then can't be bought. It can't be borrowed. It doesn't store well. And it has to have been used regularly and recently. What we will need in our day of testing is a spiritual preparation. It is to have developed faith in Jesus Christ so powerful that we can pass the test of life upon which everything for us in eternity depends. That test is part of the purpose God had for us in the Creation."

Elder Eyring then said this: "It will take *unshakable* faith in the Lord Jesus Christ to *choose* the way to eternal life" ("Spiritual Preparedness: Start Early and Be Steady," 37–38; emphasis added). Note his use of the words *unshakable* and *choose*. Note also his counsel to put the Lord first, to seek Him early, to develop in advance of trial and travail a testimony that He is the Christ.

We are experiencing in our day what appears to be a dramatic increase in violent storms that wipe out entire cities and regions in massive, destructive swipes. But the spiritual and moral tsunamis we're subjected to constantly can be even more life-threatening, and the recovery from such devastation can seem impossible. The only way to confront and avoid the complexities, confusion, and moral congestion of latter-day life is to have a testimony of Jesus Christ—His divinity, His power, and His gospel. The only safety is in coming unto Christ, which means walking away from the world.

The only way to confront and avoid the complexities, confusion, and moral congestion of latter-day life is to have a testimony of Jesus Christ—His divinity, His power, and His gospel.

We know this. This is not new news. And yet it can be difficult to do.

Last summer I attended a conference held in Salzburg, Austria, for young single adults throughout central Europe. During one session I asked these impressive young adult men and women the question, "What is turning out to be more difficult at this stage of your life than you expected it to be?" Their answers ran the gamut and included everything from adjusting after a mission, to having relatively few people to date, to finding their way in the world and knowing what careers or education they should pursue.

The very last comment came from a handsome young Austrian man who said: "I've been home from my mission for a year. I loved my mission, and I tried to do my best. I love the Lord and am so grateful for Him." Then he paused and admitted, "But what is proving to be harder for me than I ever expected is following Jesus Christ without reservation."

That perceptive young man articulated the challenge with which every one of us must deal, to at least some degree, throughout our lives: Will we follow Jesus Christ without reservation? That implies following Him without hesitation, without restraint, without taking occasional detours, without holding back. It means putting Him first, looking to Him first. The only way to fight the fire that destroys is with the fire that sanctifies.

Now, in truth, none of us are following Him *all the time* without reservation, hesitation, restraint, or holding back. To do so implies perfection—or at least near perfection. But it *is* possible to decide once and for all that we will follow Jesus Christ, meaning that we will try to live His teachings and become increasingly like Him. It is possible to become increasingly pure. It is possible to become perfectly obedient to certain commandments. For example, it is possible to be perfect in the payment of tithes. It is possible to be perfect in not consuming or even sampling pornography. It is possible to be perfectly chaste. It is possible to be perfect in repenting quickly and not allowing mistakes to fester. It is possible to be perfect in our motives and attitudes. In making these steps toward perfection by being perfect in certain things, we can increasingly learn to follow the Savior without reservation.

Elder Bruce R. McConkie suggested what this entails: "To be valiant in the testimony of Jesus is to take the Lord's side on every issue. It is to vote as he would vote. It is to think what he thinks, to believe what he believes, to say what he would say and do what he would do in the same situation. It is to have the mind of Christ and be one with him as he is one with his Father" ("Be Valiant in the Fight of Faith," 35).

We have unlimited spiritual potential if we gain our own testimony of Jesus Christ, study and learn His doctrines, and learn how to hear His voice and the voice of the Father as communicated by and through the Holy Ghost. The Father, in giving us His Plan and His Son, and the Son, in atoning for us, have given us something so much better, so much more complete, so much more filled with joy and hope and peace than anything the world has to offer.

Not long ago, while flipping through TV channels, I noticed a program on the History Channel entitled *A History of God*. Curious about how a secular program would represent God, I couldn't resist watching. One philosopher and religious historian after another opined on the subject—all of whom missed the mark and failed to speak of Him as *our Father*, the Father of our spirits. None acknowledged His omniscience. No one came even close to recognizing His grandeur and overarching power. No one even hinted at His careful and loving involvement in the lives of His children, as did Elder

Bruce R. McConkie when he taught that, while Jehovah created the earth and all forms of plant and animal life thereon, "when it came to placing man on earth, there was a change in Creators. That is, the Father himself became personally involved. All things were created by the Son, using the power delegated by the Father, except man. In the spirit and again in the flesh, man was created by the Father. There was no delegation of authority where the crowning creature of creation was concerned" (*Promised Messiah*, 62). None of the celebrated theologians commenting on God came anywhere close to describing His splendor. The statement that sent me through the roof, though, was this one: "God is a work in progress."

God is *anything* but a work in progress. He is a glorified, perfected, and exalted Being who has all might, power, and dominion. He is omniscient and omnipresent, knows all things, and is filled with perfect love and mercy. We, on the other hand, *are* works in progress. And our only hope of becoming like Him is His willingness to share all He has and all He knows with us, His children.

Every December as we enjoy the Christmas holidays, we experience a season of giving and heightened generosity. We can all call to mind countless gifts we've received

> God is anything *but a work in progress. He is a glorified, perfected, and exalted Being who has all might, power, and dominion.*

through the years and those who've remembered us with their kindness and benevolence. But when I reflect on the many individuals who have been generous with me, I rarely think of something that's gift-wrapped. Instead I think of those who have been patient with me or overlooked my weaknesses once again; who have encouraged and believed in me, even when I didn't believe in myself; who have given me the benefit of the doubt; who have taught me things I didn't understand or appreciate or know; who've given me the gift of their time; who've trusted me with challenging assignments or sensitive information; or who've dropped everything when I've been in need to counsel or support or bless me in some way. As a popular saying goes, the most important things in life are not things. Such gifts of charity are the epitome of human generosity.

The ultimate in generosity, though, is without doubt or argument the generosity of our Father and His Son. Our Father generously devised a plan whereby we may return to live with Him and even become like Him; and then, recognizing the full extent of our weaknesses and needs, He sent us His Son. And the Son generously did what He was sent to do, atoning for each and every one of us and being willing and even joyful about allowing all who qualify to become joint-heirs with Him of all the Father has. For "the Spirit itself beareth witness with our spirit, that we are the children of God: And if children, then heirs; heirs of God, and joint-heirs with Christ; if so be that we suffer with him, that we may be also glorified together." As the Apostle Paul said, "the sufferings of this present time are not worthy to be compared with the glory which shall be revealed in us" (Romans 8:16–18).

No wonder the Savior implored, "Lift up your hearts and be glad, for I am in your midst, and am your advocate with the

Father; and it is his good will to give you the kingdom" (D&C 29:5). If we will seek the riches which it is the will of the Father to give us, we "shall be the richest of all people, for [we] shall have the riches of eternity" (D&C 38:39) and "inherit all things" (D&C 78:22). That is unfettered generosity—extended to us as the result of our looking to the Lord first, early in our lives, early in the day, early in every situation.

It's too much for the mortal mind to take in, let alone comprehend. But the evidence is everywhere present—both personally and universally.

I have dear friends who have raised eight terrific children. Because the husband's work often takes him out of town—and when he *is* home, he's often attending to his responsibilities as a stake president—his wife has largely borne the brunt of running the home and caring for the children. One week while he was away, their youngest child created quite a disturbance, one that needed parental intervention. That evening, when my friend telephoned her husband to report the day's events, she said, "Remind me, why *did* we have eight children?" To which he instantly responded, "Because the Lord knew we could have handled seven just fine."

We often reassure each other that we won't tempted beyond that which we can bear. But the scriptures are actually conditional on this point. We are counseled to humble ourselves before the Lord, to call on his holy name, and to watch and pray continually so that we will not be tempted above that which we can bear. In other words, the promise is based upon our righteous actions (see Alma 13:28–29).

Further, the Lord *does* give us more than we can handle—

by ourselves, that is. He does this so that we will have every opportunity and motivation to seek Him early, to put Him first. He atoned precisely so that we would not have to shoulder our burdens or the disappointments of mortality alone.

This again from Elder Eyring: "The great test of life is . . . not to endure storms, but to choose the right while they rage. . . . We are the spirit children of a Heavenly Father. . . . He told us that He wished to give us *all that He had*. To qualify for that gift we had to receive mortal bodies and be tested. . . . We would be subject to temptations through the desires and weaknesses that came with our mortal bodies. Subtle and powerful forces of evil would tempt us to surrender to those temptations. . . . [But] we were promised that we would have Jehovah, Jesus Christ, as our Savior and Redeemer. . . . He would make it possible for us to pass the test of life if we exercised faith in Him by being obedient. We shouted for joy at the good news" ("Spiritual Preparedness: Start Early and Be Steady," 38; emphasis added).

King Benjamin taught his people the same thing. After prophesying that the Savior would come and testifying of what He would do, King Benjamin asked his people if they were willing to covenant with God to do His will and to be obedient to His commandments all of their days, to which his people responded willingly and eagerly. He then declared that because of the covenant they had made, they would be called the children of Christ, His sons and daughters, "for behold, this day he hath spiritually begotten you; for ye say that your hearts are changed through faith on his name; therefore, ye are born of him and have become his sons and his daughters. . . . There is no other name given whereby salvation cometh; therefore, I would that ye should take upon you the name of Christ" (Mosiah 5:7–8).

We speak often of coming unto Christ. We talk of Him; we preach of Him. But do we *rejoice* that He came to earth, completed His mission perfectly in Gethsemane and on Calvary, and as a result created a reservoir of spiritual strength and power from which we can draw? He *is* the living water, the "well of water springing up into everlasting life" (John 4:14). He is the only water that quenches spiritual and emotional thirst. Have we therefore determined to do our best to follow Him without reservation?

C. S. Lewis wrote that "to walk out of His [meaning the Savior's] will is to walk into nowhere" (*The Quotable Lewis*, 263). Anything short of learning how to follow Jesus Christ without reservation is like walking into nowhere. Anything short of accepting the remarkable generosity of the Father and the Son is a spiritual dead-end.

And that is because the only way to worship the Father is by following His Son. It is by putting Him first.

We can take our faith in Jesus Christ, our devotion to Him, our testimony that He is the Son of God, with us throughout eternity. And the fire of that testimony burning within our souls, the fire of having been born of the Spirit, is the only way to overcome the fires of moral and spiritual destruction raging throughout this world and the fire of eternal disappointment and damnation.

If mortals make mistakes—and we all know we do—then why are
we so often tempted to listen to the world's experts rather than the
Lord's? Why do we seem to favor earthly counsel
over that of prophets, seers, and revelators?

CHAPTER SIX

MORTALS MAKE MISTAKES

I have a dear friend who is Betty Crocker, Martha Stewart, and the Galloping Gourmet all rolled into one terrific package. She is the quintessential Hostess with the Mostess, sees life as a series of celebrations waiting to happen, and knows how to entertain and make anyone at any gathering, large or small, feel included and welcome. She's a great cook, but her talents extend far beyond the kitchen, as she has a gift for making friends feel like family. She has countless skills I don't have.

So a couple of Decembers ago, when she asked what I wanted for Christmas, I was quick to reply: "Cooking lessons," adding for good measure, "and could you also show me how you go about planning those fabulous parties you throw?" Ever the good sport, she agreed, and the lessons began.

She got me through Easter, when my family descended on my house for dinner. But a few weeks later, when they agreed to come again, this time for Mother's Day, I needed a new entree. Something I hadn't served before. Something that was foolproof. When I asked my friend what to do, she responded instantly: "Pot roast. It's not possible to ruin pot roast." She promised point-by-point instructions, right down to what cut of meat to purchase.

My friend came through with the instructions, and I studied them carefully, paying particular attention to how long I was to cook the roast: four hours on low in a Crock-Pot.

Mother's Day arrived. I followed every instruction to the letter and was feeling just a bit smug at the prospect of pulling off two great family dinners in a matter of weeks—until I checked the roast at the three-and-one-half-hour mark and knew I was in BIG TROUBLE! The meat looked as bloodred as it had when I'd put it in 210 minutes earlier. Honestly, the beef was so rare that if I'd lifted the lid it would probably have started mooing.

I panicked. Twenty-four people were even at that moment en route to my home. I tried to reach my friend, but she was (conveniently for her) still at church. So I bit the bullet and called one of my sisters. As I explained what had happened, she began to howl with laughter, instantly diagnosing the problem. When she finally regained her composure (and after she had explained to her husband, quite a chef himself, Sheri's latest cooking crisis and waited for *his* howling to subside), she said, simply, "Sheri, it would take at least twice as long to cook a roast that size in a Crock-Pot. But hang on, the cavalry is on the way. We'll help you salvage dinner."

The long story made short is that we eventually got everyone fed—not, however, without adding another of "Sheri's cooking disasters" to family lore.

What happened? It's simple: As my friend painstakingly prepared instructions, she deliberated about whether it would be easier for me to cook the pot roast in the oven, which takes less time, or the Crock-Pot. She went back and forth in her mind—and in the e-mail in which she described the step-by-step process. At the last minute, she changed her mind and opted to recommend the Crock-Pot but forgot to change the time required. Hence, a roast that was still red, red, red at serving time.

The moral of the story? *Mortals make mistakes.* Some of those mistakes are completely innocent, like my friend's, and some are not. Some are intentional, and some are not. And when you're on the receiving end of the information, it can be difficult to tell which is which. Even, as in this case, a well-meaning friend trying her best to help, even a friend with the purest of intentions, can make an honest mistake that leads you down, as it were, the garden path.

> *Even a friend with the purest of intentions can make an honest mistake that leads you down, as it were, the garden path.*

If mortals make mistakes—and we all know that we do, because we've each made plenty and so has everyone we know—then why are we so often tempted to listen to the world's experts rather than the Lord's? Why do we seem to favor earthly counsel over that of prophets, seers, and revelators as well as others called and gifted with priesthood keys, mantles, and stewardships to lead us?

There are as many answers as there are situations and human beings:

—Sometimes it seems easier to follow the world, though it never is.

—Sometimes it's hard not to get distracted by the clamor, appeal, and even allure of the world and all it has to offer.

—Sometimes we lose track of who we're listening to.

—Sometimes we're afraid to go to local priesthood leaders and may talk ourselves out of seeking counsel.

—Sometimes the entertainment or fun factor grabs us.

—Sometimes we're too proud.

—Sometimes we're lazy.

—Sometimes we're dumber than dirt. . . .

Think about it. We're promised that if we "receive the Holy Ghost, it will show unto [us] all things what [we] should do" (2 Nephi 32:5). *All things*. What a remarkably comprehensive promise! Can you think of *anyone* or *anything* on this earth that can supply the answer to all things? I asked that question in a recent institute class, and a young man trying to be smart (read, smart-aleck) said, "Yeah, Google!" That raises an interesting point. Google and other current web-based search engines present the illusion of knowing everything, or of at least being able to search a seemingly endless database of information and provide instant access to all knowledge.

But only God is endless and eternal: "Behold, I am God," He declared. "Man of Holiness is my name; Man of Counsel is my name; and Endless and Eternal is my name" (Moses 7:35). Only the Father and the Son know everything. Only They have all knowledge, all wisdom, all power. Google, on the other hand, is no different from anything else man-made in that it can search for and sort *only* the information provided by man. What Google cannot do (please note, this is *not* an attack on Google, which like other similar tools is helpful for navigating the web) is provide an assessment of which information is true and which is not. And it certainly cannot supply things of the Spirit.

Google is limited by the wisdom of its inventors—mortals who, like all humans, make mistakes. That fact prompts two obvious but compelling questions: Why, then, do we have a tendency to put the world first? And to whom are we *really* listening—the world or the Lord? Who has our ears and our hearts: the world, with its experts, celebrities, and pundits, all of whose competition for fans and followers creates a cacophony of noise; or the Lord, who speaks through the still, small voice, through the Word, and through His called servants? Although this question may seem easy to answer, a close assessment of where and how we spend our time and focus our attention may prove revealing. Case in point:

Every year the General Relief Society Meeting is held on

To whom are we really *listening—the world or the Lord?*

the Saturday evening prior to the October general conference. There is no mystery or secret about this schedule. This significant meeting is held on the same Saturday every year, lasts ninety minutes, and gives the women of the Church the opportunity to hear messages prepared specifically for them by a member of the First Presidency as well as the Relief Society general presidency. Great consideration and preparation, prayer and earnest seeking precede that meeting, and it is the only time during the year when those with a stewardship for the women of the Church speak directly and specifically to them.

One year, just a few days after the General Relief Society Meeting, I happened upon a conversation among several female colleagues who were discussing a compelling issue. After listening for a few minutes, I said, "Did you hear Sister Kathy Hughes's address at the General Relief Society Meeting this past weekend? She spoke to this very topic, and her message was superb." There were blank stares all around. Not one of those women had attended or viewed the broadcast—and this was in Utah, where it's not difficult to find. Finally one woman said, "Oh, I'll have to download that talk from lds.org and make sure I study it." Then, without even a pause, she added, "But did you see the segment on *Oprah* last week about this topic? It was terrific."

"How is that you managed to catch *Oprah?*" I asked, trying not to reveal the emotion behind the question.

"Oh," she responded, "I tape it every day and watch it at night." Come to find out, several others in that group did as well.

At that moment, there were volumes I wanted to say, none of which would have been appropriate in the workplace. But it is frightening to contemplate that such good, typically insightful, Latter-day Saint women would make such a concerted effort to tune in a celebrity but respond so casually to a meeting in which our called leaders, including a member of the First Presidency, prepare messages the Lord wishes His covenant daughters to hear. It isn't asking much, is it, to set aside ninety minutes a year to hear the voice of the Lord?

Please don't misunderstand: The world is filled with experts, scholars, and others who provide important opportunities to learn, grow, and increase in knowledge and insight. But even knowledge we accept today as truth—particularly in the sciences—will be debunked and replaced with new findings in coming years. Because mortals are just mortals. And they make mistakes.

Further, it is always dangerous to take counsel from *anyone* whose primary motive is building his or her own kingdom.

Even knowledge we accept today as truth—particularly in the sciences—will be debunked and replaced with new findings in coming years. Because mortals are just mortals. And they make mistakes.

The "authorities" the world has embraced promote concepts and ideologies that are typically nothing more or less than a mixture of the philosophies of men . . . interspersed casually with bits of truth and doctrine. A recent popular women's magazine is representative of countless others. Several articles on building relationships and improving one's health looked helpful. But included in the same issue was an article entitled "You Gotta Have Faith: It Doesn't Have to Be a God Thing." One wonders, then, faith in what? Or whom? Anything less than faith in God the Father and Jesus Christ is merely a superficial kind of confidence.

Anything less than faith in God the Father and Jesus Christ is merely a superficial kind of confidence.

Abraham Lincoln learned to not trust in the arm of flesh. In June 1863, just prior to the battle of Gettysburg, Lincoln was asked if he felt the country would survive. "I do not doubt that our country will finally come through safe and undivided," President Lincoln responded. "But do not misunderstand me. . . . I do not rely on the patriotism of our people . . . the bravery and devotion of the boys in blue . . . (or) the loyalty and skill of our generals. . . . But the God of our fathers . . . will bring us through safe" (Federer, *America's God and Country*, 384–85). Later, as General Robert E. Lee led his Confederate army of 76,000 men into Pennsylvania, panic raced through Washington, D. C. Through it all, Lincoln remained confident. He later admitted that "when everyone seemed panic-stricken . . . I went to my room . . . and got down on my knees before

Almighty God and prayed. . . . Soon a sweet comfort crept into my soul that God Almighty had taken the whole business into His own hands" (*America's God and Country*, 385).

Again, to whom are we listening: the world or the Lord? C. S. Lewis said it this way: "Never, never pin your whole faith on any human being: not if he is the best and wisest in the whole world. There are lots of nice things you can do with sand: but do not try building a house on it" (*Mere Christianity*, 163).

Isaiah's warning on this matter is sobering: "Woe to the rebellious children, saith the Lord, that take counsel, but not of me; and that cover with a covering, but not of my spirit, that they may add sin to sin" (Isaiah 30:1). Isaiah's statement raises two obvious questions: From whom are we taking our counsel? And are we focused on being filled with the Spirit of the Lord so we can detect between right and wrong, between truth and error?

Foreseeing our day, Nephi prophesied that churches would be built up and their priests would contend with one another, teaching their own learning while denying "the Holy Ghost, which giveth utterance." He testified that these latter-day religionists would deny the power of God and exhort the masses to listen to them, saying there was no longer a God involved in the affairs of men, "for the Lord and the Redeemer hath done his work." He then warned, "Wo be unto him that hearkeneth unto the precepts of men, and denieth the power of God, and the gift of the Holy Ghost" (2 Nephi 28:4–5, 26).

Through the Prophet Joseph Smith, the Lord counseled

the Saints of this dispensation to "pray always, that you may come off conqueror; yea, that you may conquer Satan, and that you may escape the hands of the servants of Satan that do uphold his work" (D&C 10:5). All around us are those who uphold Satan's work. Some who do so are no doubt aware of what they're doing; others are only his pawns. Unfortunately, the impact on those Lucifer controls is largely the same, which makes it all the more crucial that we know the doctrines of the gospel of Jesus Christ.

President James E. Faust said this about the adversary's approach and allure: "Who has not heard and felt the enticing of the devil? His voice often sounds so reasonable and his message so easy to justify. It is an appealing, intriguing voice with dulcet tones. It is neither hard nor discordant. No one would listen to Satan's voice if it sounded harsh or mean. If the devil's voice were unpleasant, it would not persuade people to listen to it" ("The Forces That Will Save Us," 6).

The Savior liberates,

while Satan captivates,

then captures.

Nonetheless, and despite Lucifer's varied strategies—subtle and otherwise—to trick and trap us, the differences between his way, or the way of the world, and the way of the Lord are actually in many respects dramatic. Consider the following distinctions:

The Savior liberates, while Satan captivates, then captures.

The Lord gives us commandments to keep and covenants to make that liberate us because they keep us from enslavement.

Lucifer claims that he's all about freedom, but everything he does enslaves. He binds us with his cords and chains, holding us hostage with everything from the bondage of debt to the bondage of addiction. He ensnares us in everything from pornography to prescription medications to money and power.

The Lord gave us our agency to choose; Lucifer tried to force us to do it his way.

The Lord is selfless—His atonement was entirely for us; Satan is the epitome of arrogance and selfishness, so much so that he even desires us to be miserable as he is.

The Lord is inclusive and has declared again and again that *all* who qualify may receive *all* that He has. His atonement was infinite and eternal—meaning that no matter how much healing or saving or sanctifying one person needs, there is plenty to go around for all others who seek and qualify. Lucifer is the ultimate exclusionist and is behind everything that seeks to put one person ahead of another. He is playing the ultimate game of "Survival," and he wants us to believe that only a few can win and therefore that anything it takes to "get ahead" is justified.

The Lord communicates His will through the still, small voice; Lucifer is the master of noise, commotion, and confusion.

The Lord communicates His will through the still, small voice; Lucifer is the master of noise, commotion, and confusion.

The Lord created a world of breathtaking beauty and tranquility where everything in nature and life works together to create balance. Satan takes the joy and beauty out of everything. Life is better, nature is better, humankind is better than Satan ever portrays them to be. As just one obvious example, he reduces intimacy to a base, carnal desire to be exploited, whereas our Father gave this beautiful expression of love to His sons and daughters to allow them to participate in the miracle of creation and take a step closer to godhood.

The Lord will fill us with peace, whereas Lucifer works full-time with his minions to discourage, disrupt, depress, and fill us with despair.

The Lord is about endless lives. Satan is about endless misery.

The Lord is the Master Healer and will heal our emotions, our spirits, our souls, our sins (if we repent), and even our bodies. Lucifer, who is the personification of communicable spiritual disease, tries to infect us with the spiritual maladies of sin, selfishness, and pride.

The Lord will fill us with peace, whereas Lucifer works full-time with his minions to discourage, disrupt, depress, and fill us with despair.

There is one thing the Lord and Lucifer have in common: *They both desire us to become as they are.* The Lord wants us to become like He is: a God, with eternal lives, endless power, endless posterity, and "never-ending happiness" (Mosiah 2:41), and beloved by His children.

Satan, who epitomizes the phrase "misery loves company," also wants us to become as he is—miserable, filthy, unembodied, without family or posterity, a creature without hope or a future, incapable of feeling joy, despised by all who know him—someone who is completely and utterly alone.

It's not much of a contest, is it?

Parley P. Pratt described to his wife Belinda the utter loneliness he felt while traveling to England on the *Queen of the West*. On October 1, 1846, about eleven hundred miles from New York City, he wrote: "I am Alone!—Alone!—Alone! O Horrible!—Yes—Alone—the punishment—the Hell I always dread—and the one to which I am often doomed. How oft has it been my lot to spend wearisome days, weeks and even months, confined to the society of those whose spirits, ways, manners, tastes, pursuits, hopes and destiny are so different from mine, that not a single chord, or nerve beats in unison. This is hell to me. I pray the Lord to deliver me from such torment and to grant me one thing above all others; and that is: the privilege of enjoying the society of kindred spirits" (Proctor, *Autobiography of Parley P. Pratt*, 437, n. 15).

One of the remarkable distinctions between our Father and Lucifer is that our Father and those who follow Him will enjoy endless, even eternal posterity and associations. Lucifer, on the other hand, will reap the torment of an endless, eternal damnation, and each of his followers will face that damnation alone.

Loneliness is the epitome of misery. If my only motivation were to avoid eternal loneliness, that would be enough to convince me to keep the commandments. But happily, our Father has offered us so much more than just the chance to avoid negative consequences. He has offered to tell us everything He knows and to share everything He has with His Son and with us.

And yet, we are too often too easily beguiled by the world—by the latest fashions, the latest trends and gadgets, the latest round of celebrities, the latest MVP, the latest glib reporter or anchorman or talk-show host, the latest political icon.

At least as dangerous as anything yet mentioned, and perhaps more so, is the threat of falling prey to the philosophies of man. As one example, these days the adversary is attacking and creating confusion about everything central to the plan of salvation, including issues related to gender, marriage, the family as the Lord intended it, womanhood and motherhood, and manhood and fatherhood as the Lord defined them. Lucifer is working overtime to undermine and even eradicate the need for marriage, to emasculate men, and to portray women as trivial objects without influence. Check any newsstand, or the programming on just about any TV channel—you won't find examples of divinely appointed manhood or womanhood. Men were foreordained to "bear the vessels of the Lord" (D&C 38:42), having been "prepared from eternity

Surely there is nothing more beautiful in the eyes of the Lord than a holy man who is riveted on becoming like his Father, and a pure woman who is filled with the Holy Ghost.

to all eternity, according to his foreknowledge of all things" to be ordained to the high priesthood (see Alma 13:7–10). Likewise, women were foredesignated and positioned at the very center of the plan of salvation, endowed with the privilege of bearing and nurturing in mortality our Father's own spirit sons and daughters. Surely there is nothing more beautiful in the eyes of the Lord than a holy man who is riveted on becoming like his Father, and a pure woman who is filled with the Holy Ghost.

And yet Lucifer tries to emasculate men, often portraying them as simple, mindless creatures who care only about the pleasures of the flesh. And he does everything imaginable to undermine motherhood and pure womanhood, shouting that a woman's essence and value are measured entirely by her physical appeal, and that, if anything, motherhood threatens her image as well as her womanly wiles.

Men and women never recover from living beneath themselves. Men and women never recover from turning their backs on their divinely appointed gifts and roles.

Motherhood is at the very heart of a woman's divine nature. I know this is true. I know it because the doctrine is clear on this point. And I know it because I cannot imagine ever getting over not bearing children in this life. I have the consolation, or at least reassurance, that the Lord has directed my life and that it is in accordance with His mind and will, but that doesn't ease the pain of not bearing children. And I can testify to the emptiness that comes from trying so hard, for so long, to find a companion and begin a family, and yet finding that dream unfulfilled—and coming to the stark realization that part of that dream can never be fulfilled in this life. If I believed that this life were the end, the sense of gloom and doom would be too much to bear.

Satan would have men and women become enthralled with the glitter and glories of the world, all of which fade away faster than yesterday's news. Nothing the world can offer has the enduring joy of eternal motherhood and fatherhood. Period. You'll never hear that on a sitcom or read it in a popular magazine. And that's why it's vital that we listen to the Lord and His servants on these and all crucial issues rather than the glib philosophies of man.

The kingdom of God would change overnight if latter-day men and women of God understood who they are and what their commission is.

The kingdom of God would change overnight if latter-day men and women of God understood who they are and what their commission is, and if we could unlock the influence of holy men and pure women, working together to build His kingdom. The number of missionaries would increase, more prospective elders would become elders, more men and women would find more time to worship the Lord in the House of the Lord, tithes and offerings would increase, more families would be stronger, and on and on. But you won't hear that message from the world.

How many magazines or sitcoms or DVDs portray *any* of the following truths:

—That all human beings, male and female, are created in the image of God.

—That each of us has a divine nature and destiny.

—That God's commandment to multiply and replenish the earth remains in force.

—That the sacred powers of procreation are to be employed and expressed only between man and woman, lawfully wedded as husband and wife.

—That parents have a sacred duty toward their children.

—That the family is ordained of God, and that marriage between man and woman is essential to God's eternal plan.

—That fathers are to preside over their families, provide for them, and protect them.

—That mothers are primarily responsible for the nurture of their children.

—That mothers and fathers are equal partners.

—That individuals who violate covenants of chastity, who abuse spouse or offspring, or who fail to fulfill family responsibilities will stand accountable before God.

—Or that the disintegration of the family will bring upon individuals, communities, and nations the calamities foretold by prophets ancient and modern (see "The Family: A Proclamation to the World").

Sadly, in only the rarest of instances does today's public commentary embrace any of those truths. Foreseeing our era, Nephi prophesied that the day would come when we would be susceptible to the perils of the Five Ps: to Pride; to "getting gain," or Possessions; to gaining Power; to becoming Popular; and to seeking the lusts or Pleasures of the flesh (see 1 Nephi 22:23). The active pursuit of possessions, power, popularity, or pleasures of the flesh, often motivated by pride, can drown out the still, small voice, momentarily overshadow truth, and distract us from those things that bring real joy and lasting happiness.

The active pursuit of possessions, power, popularity, or pleasures of the flesh, often motivated by pride, can drown out the still, small voice, momentarily overshadow truth, and distract us from those things that bring real joy and lasting happiness.

Lucifer has actively promoted these perils, with recurring success, again and again, including during the time prior to the Crucifixion. In just a few years, the more part of the Nephites slipped from righteousness into wickedness because "Satan had great power, unto the stirring up of the people to do all manner of iniquity, and to the puffing them up with pride, tempting them to seek for power, and authority, and riches, and the vain things of the world" (3 Nephi 6:15). Again, depravity and iniquity are the inevitable result of the natural man's thirst for Pride, Power, Popularity, Possessions, and Pleasures of the flesh.

Both taking counsel from man and doing things to be seen of man are spiritual dead-ends.

The natural consequence of yielding oneself to Lucifer's antics was aptly demonstrated by Korihor, the anti-Christ, who ridiculed the believers, proclaiming that there was no God, no penalty for sinning, no Christ, and no Atonement, and in the process "leading away the hearts of many, causing them to lift up their heads in their wickedness" (Alma 30:18). Korihor had a heyday among the Nephites, deceiving them, distracting them, and leading many toward spiritual death. The people of Ammon, formerly Lamanites, were wiser. When Korihor came among them, they carried him before Ammon, the high priest, who evicted him from the land, giving the righteous of all eras a pattern to emulate. The only way to deal with Satan is to evict him and not give him or his temptations opportunity to take hold.

> *The only way to deal with Satan is to evict him and not give him or his temptations opportunity to take hold.*

Further, when Korihor then went into the land of Gideon, again he was bound and taken before the high priest, who said these simple but profound words: "Why do ye go about perverting the ways of the Lord? Why do ye teach this people that there shall be no Christ, *to interrupt their rejoicings?*" (Alma 30:22; emphasis added).

Plain and simple, the enticements, the lies, the flatteries of Satan interrupt our rejoicings, for happiness and peace and joy come in and through the Lord Jesus Christ, who taught a sermon in one verse when He promised: "Peace I leave with you, my peace I give unto you; *not as the world giveth, give I unto you*. Let not your heart be troubled, neither let it be afraid" (John 14:27; emphasis added). The Savior gifts us with peace and healing and wholeness in a way the world can never duplicate.

Coming unto Christ means walking away from the world.

That process isn't easy, and it isn't automatic. But, said C. S. Lewis, that should not rob of us hope: "God knows quite well how hard we find it to love Him more than anyone or anything else, and He won't be angry with us as long as we are trying. And He will help us" (*The Quotable Lewis*, 409).

In the temple we learn how to come out of the world, meaning the telestial nature of this mortal probation, by living a higher, holier law. And if we want to have the ability, even the power, to take the gospel of Jesus Christ into all the world, we must first as followers of Him come out of the world.

Again, the world is a spiritual dead-end. Elder Bruce R. McConkie left no doubt about that. "Here is a truism that all men should hear," he wrote. "Babylon [which is prophetic imagery for the world] fell, and her gods with her; and Babylon shall fall, and her gods with her. False gods create an evil society. The world is the world, and Babylon is Babylon, because they worship false gods. When men worship the true God according to gospel standards, their social conditions rival those in Enoch's city; when men worship false gods, they fall into the ways of the world" (*Millennial Messiah*, 429–30).

Babylon, or the world, is a spiritual dead-end because mortals make mistakes. Some mistakes are innocent, others are not.

Our Father, on the other hand, knows all, understands all, and never makes mistakes. As we strive to focus on and follow His Son, we will be blessed with an ever greater measure of His power.

For each of us, a testimony that Joseph was a prophet is crucial, for if he was the Lord's anointed, then the gospel is true and the Lord's own Church was restored to the earth. If he wasn't a prophet, then the gospel is simply a wise way to live.

CHAPTER SEVEN

POWER AND THE RESTORATION

Any discussion of the Lord's power, and what we must do to qualify for and access that power, would be pointless were it not for the Restoration.

God chose a humble and even, by the world's standards, obscure farm boy, a young man nonetheless "called up to serious reflection and great uneasiness" about religion (JS–H 1:8), to usher in the final dispensation by restoring the ancient Church of Jesus Christ and His priesthood to the earth. "This restoration was to be the last," taught Elder Robert D. Hales, "the dispensation of the fulness of times, restoring all the priesthood blessings which man could possess on earth. With this divine commission, his work was not to reform nor was it to protest what was already on the earth. It was to restore what had been on earth and had been lost" ("Preparations for the Restoration and the Second Coming," 91).

The Prophet Joseph Smith became a living witness that the

heavens are open and that God, our Father, will communicate with us. The heavens opened in dramatic fashion that beautiful spring morning when the teenage Joseph knelt in prayer, seeking to know which church to join. The theophany that then occurred in that sacred grove of trees in upstate New York was both unexpected and transcendent. Instructed to join none of the existing churches, Joseph also learned why: "They draw near to me with their lips," said a glorious Personage whose brightness and glory defied all description, "but their hearts are far from me, they teach for doctrines the commandments of men, having a form of godliness, but they *deny the power thereof*" (JS–H 1:19; emphasis added).

Surely the Lord is offended with those who question or deny His power. Surely He mourns for those who reject His offer of spiritual gifts and endowments.

After centuries of spiritual and religious decay and darkness, during which those who professed religion had universally rejected the power of God, the Church of Jesus Christ would be restored in its fulness and the authority and keys and power to act in God's name and to perform sacred, redeeming ordinances would once again be given to a prophet on the earth.

Surely the Lord is offended with those who question or deny His power. Surely He mourns for those who reject His offer of spiritual gifts and endowments.

How serious are the ramifications for those who deny the

Lord's power? Mormon left no doubt about the penalty for unbelievers: "Wo unto him that shall deny the Christ and his works! Yea, wo unto him that shall deny the revelations of the Lord, and that shall say the Lord no longer worketh by revelation, or by prophecy, or by gifts, or by tongues, or by healings, or by the power of the Holy Ghost! Yea, and wo unto him that shall say at that day . . . that there can be no miracle wrought by Jesus Christ; for he that doeth this shall become like unto the son of perdition, for whom there was no mercy, according to the word of Christ!" (3 Nephi 29:5–7).

Joseph's First Vision returned to the world a firsthand witness of God, His Son, and Their power. Referring to that occurrence as the greatest event "since the birth, life, death, and Resurrection of our Lord in the meridian of time," President Gordon B. Hinckley put it in further context: "For centuries men . . . argued concerning the nature of Deity. . . . [Joseph] simply says that God stood before him and spoke to him. Joseph could see Him and could hear Him. He was in form like a man, a being of substance. Beside Him was the resurrected Lord, a separate being, whom He introduced as His Beloved Son and with whom Joseph also spoke. I submit that in the short time of that remarkable vision Joseph learned more concerning Deity than all of the scholars and clerics of the past. In this divine revelation there was reaffirmed beyond doubt the reality of the literal Resurrection of the Lord Jesus Christ" ("The Great Things Which God Has Revealed," 81).

In the days and years following the First Vision, the Savior would make manifest His power again and again to and through the young Joseph. The sheer number of visions, heavenly manifestations, and revelations the young prophet received during his brief thirty-eighty and a half years of life would prove to be staggering. "It is my meditation all the day, and more than my meat and drink, to know how I shall make the Saints of God comprehend the visions that roll like an overflowing surge before my mind," he said in 1843, more than two decades after the First Vision (*History of the Church,* 5:362).

From and through Joseph Smith we learn several principles:

First, we learn that the heavens are open, that God will talk to His children. To the Prophet Joseph, He spoke frequently. One scholar estimates that Joseph had at least seventy-six documented visionary experiences (see Welch, *Opening the Heavens,* 265). President George Q. Cannon taught that during the years prior to Joseph's receiving the plates in September 1827, he was "visited constantly by angels. . . . He had vision after vision in order that his mind might be fully saturated with a knowledge of the things of God, and that he might comprehend the great and holy calling that God has bestowed upon him" (*Journal of Discourses,* 23:362).

President John Taylor elaborated on this point: "The principles which [Joseph] had, placed him in communication with the Lord, and not only with the Lord, but with the ancient apostles and prophets; such men, for instance, as Abraham, Isaac, Jacob, Noah, Adam, Seth, Enoch, and . . . the apostles that lived on this continent as well as those who lived on the

Asiatic continent. He seemed to be as familiar with these people as we are with one another. Why? Because he had to introduce a dispensation which was called the dispensation of the fulness of times" (*Journal of Discourses*, 21:94).

Second, from and through the Prophet Joseph, we learn that God does indeed want a powerful people—meaning, a people who know how to have access to His power for the benefit of their own lives as well as those they lead and serve. Priesthood is the authority to act in God's name, and that authority is the keystone of any religion.

Third, through the Prophet Joseph we know that God will reveal *all* mysteries. When we qualify and seek, He is willing in His due time to teach us everything. Consider the breadth and depth of the Lord's promises to us through a revelation contained in just a few verses from Section 76 of the Doctrine and Covenants, verses exemplified by the Prophet. The Lord promised that He will:

—honor those who serve Him in righteousness and truth to the end,

—gift them with eternal glory,

—reveal *all* mysteries,

—reveal the wonders of eternity, including those of many generations,

—bless us with wisdom that shall be great and understanding that reaches heaven,

—enlighten us by His Spirit, and by His power make known unto us the secrets of His will, even things which eye has not seen, nor ear heard, nor yet have entered into the heart of man (see D&C 76:5–10).

Of one such vision, Joseph declared, "I could explain a hundred fold more than I ever have of the glories of the kingdoms manifested to me in the vision, were I permitted, and were the people prepared to receive them" (*History of the Church*, 5:402). Indeed, God will teach us everything, in due time. For, as Joseph taught, "The Lord deals with this people as a tender parent with a child, communicating light and intelligence and the knowledge of his ways as they can bear it" (*History of the Church*, 5:402).

Fourth, from Joseph we learn that ultimately God will give us everything—*if* we qualify.

And fifth, we learn that because the gospel has been restored to the earth, we are not alone in this vale of tears.

Because the gospel has been restored to the earth, we are not alone in this vale of tears.

Church leaders and gospel scholars have written volumes about the life, teachings, and prophetic calling of Joseph Smith, and many more volumes will no doubt follow. This brief chapter does not presume or attempt to provide a comprehensive view of the Prophet's life or ministry. Suffice it to say that a discussion of God's desires for His people wouldn't be even conceivable were it not for the Restoration and him through whom the gospel was restored.

The Lord gives us exemplars and patterns to follow, with

no exemplar or pattern in this dispensation being more instructive than the life and ministry of Joseph Smith. If we look only at his history, in particular the account canonized as scripture in the Pearl of Great Price, we learn many lessons supporting the five truths mentioned above. Consider the following:

1. *God knows who we are, where we are, what our mission is, and exactly what we need to accomplish that mission.*

In his history, Joseph Smith mentions that his father left the state of Vermont and moved his family to Palmyra, New York. One of the reasons their crops had failed yet again, driving them away from Vermont, occurred half a world away. In October 1815, an enormous volcano erupted in present-day Indonesia. The eruption sent so much ash into the atmosphere that when it reached North America the following summer, it had a cataclysmic impact on the climate and therefore on farmers. As just one example of the volcano's global effects, on June 6, 1816, it snowed in Vermont, and three days later there was a foot of snow throughout the state. Crops were destroyed. Vermonters have called that year "Eighteen hundred and froze to death."

Joseph Smith Sr. had already dealt with a series of financial reversals and agricultural disappointments, but the summer of 1816 proved to be the final blow. He moved his family to upstate New York, where they bought a farm near the Hill Cumorah.

Said Brigham Young about his mentor, the Prophet Joseph: "It was decreed in the councils of eternity, long before the foundations of the earth were laid, that he [Joseph Smith] should be the man, in the last dispensation of this world, to bring forth the word of God to the people, and receive the fulness of the keys and power of the Priesthood of the Son of God. The Lord had his eye upon him, and upon his father, and upon his father's father, and upon their progenitors clear back to Abraham, and from Abraham to the flood, and from the flood to Enoch, and from Enoch to Adam. He has watched that family and that blood as it has circulated from its fountain to the birth of that man. He was foreordained in eternity to preside over this last dispensation" (*Journal of Discourses*, 7:289–90).

Clearly God knew where Joseph was and where He needed him to be.

Further, though Joseph referred to himself as "an obscure boy . . . of no consequence" (JS–H 1:22), nothing could have been further from the truth. God the Father called Joseph by name (JS–H 1:17), as did Moroni and many other heavenly messengers (JS–H 1:33). Just as God knew Saul's name and Enoch's, Nephi's and Moroni's, Samuel's and Daniel's, He knew Joseph's. And He also knew He could count on him.

Key Learnings: Likewise, God knows our names. He chose us to come now, during the eleventh hour and the *last* time He is calling laborers into His vineyard (see D&C 33:3). He chose

> *God knows our names.*
>
> *He chose us to come now,*
>
> *during the eleventh hour*
>
> *and the last time He is*
>
> *calling laborers into*
>
> *His vineyard.*

us to come now because, among other things, He knew He could count on us to do what we promised to do in mortality. He knows where we are as well as where He needs us to be.

2. *Satan is the father of contention, confusion, pride, and anger. The only way to counteract the confusion of Lucifer is to seek the Lord.*

So contentious and confusing were the claims of various ministers and religions to the boy Joseph that he found it impossible "for a person young as I was, and so unacquainted with men and things, to come to any certain conclusion who was right and who was wrong" (JS–H 1:8). After reading the familiar passage in James, Joseph realized he must "either remain in darkness and confusion, or else . . . do as James directs, that is, ask of God" (JS–H 1:13), which he did, with life-changing, even dispensation-inaugurating results.

There would be subsequent times when he would experience anew the impact of contention. David Whitmer reported a familiar episode that took place while Joseph was in Fayette translating the Book of Mormon. Joseph was "put out about . . . something that Emma, his wife, had done." As a result, he couldn't "translate a single syllable. He went downstairs, out into the orchard, and made supplication to the Lord; was gone about an hour—came back to the house, and asked Emma's forgiveness and then came upstairs where we were and the translation went on all right" (B. H. Roberts, *Comprehensive History,* 1:131).

Key Learnings: Contention impedes the Spirit. Whenever there is confusion, contention, or darkness, Satan is present and exercising influence. The only effective response is to seek the Lord.

3. The word of God opens the windows of heaven.

The scriptures are a conduit for revelation. When Joseph read the passage in James promising that those who lacked wisdom and asked of God would be rewarded liberally (see James 1:5), he was struck with the impact of that promise. "Never did any passage of scripture come with more power to the heart of man than this did at this time to mine," he recorded. "It seemed to enter with great force into every feeling of my heart. . . . If any person needed wisdom from God, I did. . . . I at length came to the determination to 'ask of God,' concluding that if he gave wisdom to them that lacked wisdom, and would give liberally, and not upbraid, I might venture" (JS–H 1:12–13). Venture he did. In very fact, Joseph's reading of the scriptures triggered the Restoration.

Later, when Moroni appeared to Joseph, the angel quoted Old Testament prophecies. The scriptures were again integral to the work of the kingdom.

The coming forth of the Book of Mormon would prove to be at the very center of the Restoration, for it would be a key to the conversion of millions of members of the latter-day Church.

Key Learning: The scriptures are a conduit for revelation and open the windows of heaven.

4. Faith is the key to gaining access to the power of God.

Joseph took the Lord at His word. Despite having never before attempted to pray vocally, he went into the grove, *nothing doubting,* and offered up the desires of his heart to God (see JS–H 1:14–15). Surely his complete faith in the Lord's willingness to answer his prayer made it possible for the Father and the Son to respond in the manner they did.

Some three years later, worried about his "foolish errors" (JS–H 1:28), Joseph went before the Lord again, this time to know of his "state and standing before him," having *"full confidence* in obtaining a divine manifestation" (JS–H 1:29; emphasis added). In response, Moroni appeared to him not once but four times, teaching him, counseling him, and telling him about the gold plates deposited in a nearby hill.

The scriptures are a conduit for revelation and open the windows of heaven.

Throughout his life, Joseph walked by faith. As just one example, the obligation of translating the Book of Mormon could have been paralyzing for someone untrained in ancient language. But he approached the assignment with transforming faith, knowing the Lord would sustain him. In 1856 Emma described her role of writing down part of the translation as Joseph "dictated each sentence, word for word, and when he came to proper names he could not pronounce, or long words, he spelled them out, and while I was writing them, if I made a mistake in spelling, he would stop me and correct my spelling, although it was impossible for him to see how I was writing them down at the time. . . . One time while he was translating he stopped suddenly, pale as a sheet, and said, 'Emma, did

Jerusalem have walls around it?' When I answered, 'Yes,' he replied, 'Oh! I was afraid I had been deceived.' He had such a limited knowledge of history at that time that he did not even know that Jerusalem was surrounded by walls'" (Edmund C. Briggs, "A Visit to Nauvoo in 1856," *Journal of History*, October 1916; as quoted in Welch, *Opening the Heavens*, 85).

Surely every new experience with the Lord and others who ministered to him bolstered Joseph's faith that the Lord would continue to guide him and the Saints. Remarkable, even miraculous, experiences notwithstanding, Joseph did not assume that his faith in the Lord meant he wouldn't have trials. It was his faith that enabled him to deal with the disappointments, heartaches, and tribulation.

Remarkable, even miraculous, experiences notwithstanding, Joseph did not assume that his faith in the Lord meant he wouldn't have trials. It was his faith that enabled him to deal with the disappointments, heartaches, and tribulation.

Key Learning: Every spiritual experience, every answer to prayer, every spiritual confirmation should increase our confidence, our faith, that God knows who we are and that He will respond to our needs. Faith is not a bulwark against tribulation, but an assurance that the Lord is overseeing all.

5. *Satan has marvelous power, but the power of Jesus Christ is far greater.*

What happened to Joseph in the Sacred Grove is instructive for us all. Scarcely had he begun to pray when he was seized upon by an astounding power that completely overcame him, binding his tongue and surrounding him in thick darkness such that he felt "doomed to sudden destruction."

Exerting all of his power to call upon God to deliver him, and ready to sink into despair and abandon himself to destruction—"to the power of some actual being from the unseen world, who had such marvelous power" as he'd never before experienced—he saw a pillar of light greater than the brightness of the sun exactly over his head. As soon as it appeared, Joseph was delivered from "the enemy which held [him] bound," at which time he saw "two Personages, whose brightness and glory defy all description" (JS–H 1:15–17).

Satan will do anything he can to destroy the messengers of God. Joseph learned this in the grove. Further, Lucifer works feverishly to thwart any and all efforts to build the kingdom. But the light of the Father and the Son are more powerful than the darkness of the adversary; the instant they appeared, Satan had no choice but to leave.

Darkness comes in many ways. It comes in the form of discouragement and despair, heartache and loneliness, deception and distraction. It accompanies sin, particularly intentional sin. Joseph was not strong enough to contend with Satan alone, and neither are we. But the power of Jesus Christ is stronger than any kind of darkness we can expect to experience in this world, and when His power is called upon, Lucifer has no choice but to depart.

Key Learnings: Never trust those who deny the power of God. As dark and discouraging and difficult as things can become, the light or power of Jesus Christ is stronger than the darkness or power of Satan. The young Joseph showed us the way by instinctively and instantly calling upon God to deliver him, which He did. And He will deliver us.

6. *God trusts and talks to the weak and simple, including youth.*

The Lord commanded His servant Joseph to "be not weary in well-doing, for ye are laying the foundation of a great work. And out of small things proceedeth that which is great. Behold, the Lord requireth the heart and a willing mind" (D&C 64:33–34).

This principle—that the Lord uses the weak and simple to accomplish a great work—was demonstrated in Joseph's life again and again. He didn't come from a prominent family or leading city. He had no impressive degrees or wealth to back him up. He was not a wise, mature man. Joseph was but fourteen when he saw the Father and the Son, just seventeen when Moroni visited him, only twenty-one when he was entrusted with the gold plates and their translation, and just twenty-four when he organized the Church. In other words, a young adult was the first President of the Church in this dispensation.

This pattern is not unusual with the Lord, who rather than looking upon outward appearances "looketh on the heart" (1 Samuel 16:7). Moroni was just twenty-five when he became chief captain of the Nephite armies. Mormon was only fifteen when he was "visited of the Lord, and tasted and knew of the goodness of Jesus" (Mormon 1:15). Nephi was "exceedingly young" when he had "great desires to know of the mysteries of God," cried unto the Lord, and the Lord "did visit" him (1 Nephi 2:16). Enoch was "but a lad" when the Lord called him to preach repentance to the people (Moses 6:31). Heber J. Grant was only twenty-five when he was called to the Quorum of the Twelve Apostles.

Key Learnings: As President Thomas S. Monson has often said, "The Lord qualifies those whom He calls to His service." God's measure of greatness, of leadership, and of those called to serve is far different from the world's measure. Among other things, the Lord trusts youth and young adults to carry His work forward.

7. *Those who are converted to Jesus Christ must stand as witnesses of Him at all times and in all things and in all places. Sometimes that means standing alone.*

Joseph Smith spent a great deal of his life standing alone. Friends turned their backs on him. Trusted confidants and even some of his Brethren betrayed him. His own words are poignant: "So it was with me. I had actually seen a light, and in the midst of that light I saw two Personages, and they did in reality speak to me; and though I was hated and persecuted for saying that I had seen a vision, yet it was true. . . . I knew it, and I knew that God knew it, and I could not deny it, neither dared I do it" (JS–H 1:25).

> *God's measure of greatness, of leadership, and of those called to serve is far different from the world's measure.*

Those anxiously engaged in the Lord's work can expect to encounter opposition, and often the opposition from inside is greater than from without. Joseph learned this firsthand. He buried children, lost jobs and homes, endured during some periods a vagabond-like existence, and survived one false accusation and imprisonment after another. Consider just one small incident that demonstrates the daily nature of his life:

Around May 10, 1829, as Joseph and Oliver were translating, they ran out of provisions and determined to journey to Colesville to seek the help of Joseph Knight. Joseph Smith wrote of that trip: "When I first commenced this work, and had got two or three individuals to believe, I went about thirty miles with Oliver Cowdery, to see them. We had only one horse between us. When we arrived, a mob of about one hundred men came upon us before we had time to eat, and chased us all night; and we arrived back again [in Harmony] a little after daylight, having traveled about sixty miles in all, and without food" (*History of the Church*, 5:219). This is just *one* minor incident that occurred *one* night, but it is representative of the upheaval with which Joseph dealt almost daily.

Some episodes of his life were more painful. After nearly four months in Liberty Jail, he cried to the Lord, "O God, where art thou? And where is the pavilion that covereth thy hiding place? How long shall thy hand be stayed? . . . O Lord, how long shall [thy people] suffer these wrongs and unlawful oppressions" (D&C 121:1–3). Indeed, as the Lord promised him, the ends of the earth would inquire after his name, fools would have him in derision, and hell would rage against him, while the pure in heart would seek counsel and authority and blessings constantly from under his hand (see D&C 122:1–2).

Again and again, Joseph experienced the loneliness of leadership, the weight of the dispensation upon his shoulders, and the trials and tribulations that always accompany, to some degree, choosing the right and building the kingdom. Elder Robert S. Wood of the Seventy summarized the phenomenon this way: "It is wrong to assume that the more righteous one is, or the more diligently one strives to keep his or her covenants with the Lord, the less suffering one will have to endure. The promise is that he or she will be blessed, though the blessing may be the strength to endure suffering. All suffer—the just and the unjust. But the unjust live as well with the consequences of their own sins. This is the way life is arranged. God does not sit around wondering what test to throw up before you next. Such tests are integral to life—they go with the territory" (*The Complete Christian*, 95).

Joseph described his own experience when he wrote that "a religion that does not require the sacrifice of all things never has power sufficient to produce the faith necessary unto life and salvation" (*Lectures on Faith*, 6:7). He learned what the Lord understands and what every leader—whether a parent or a priesthood or auxiliary leader or the head of an organization—comes to understand, that it is easier to motivate someone to do something difficult than to do something easy, and that we are willing to give our all when we know the cause is just and right.

Certainly this is how the Lord works with us. He has

required us to do something unbelievably difficult—in working out our salvation as we overcome the world—and yet those committed to following Him are willing and able to do it.

Key Learnings: True followers of Jesus Christ have already made the choice to stand up for what we believe. All disciples of Christ can expect to have times when they must stand as witnesses of the Savior. And inevitably, there will be times when we must stand alone. It is the burden of leadership imposed upon those who have taken upon themselves the name of Christ.

All disciples of Christ can expect to have times when they must stand as witnesses of the Savior. And inevitably, there will be times when we must stand alone.

8. *Critics seize every opportunity to demean the Lord's anointed, focusing on any perceived weakness.*

Even prophets experience a normal pattern of progression, meaning that they make mistakes, repent, try again, triumph over adversity or weakness, and move forward—just as each of us must do. The young Joseph lamented the foibles of his youth, acknowledging that he was "guilty of levity, and sometimes associated with jovial company, etc., not consistent with that character which ought to be maintained by one who was called of God as [he] had been" (JS–H 1:28).

In today's world, where Lucifer's servants unleash constant attacks on the Church, and where information circles the globe instantly, it is inevitable that we will come in contact with those trying to discredit Joseph Smith. He was warned that his name would be had for good and evil among all nations, kindreds, tongues, and peoples (see JS–H 1:33). President Gordon B. Hinckley commented on this reality: "Critics, [and] not a few, . . . have worn out their lives trying . . . to find some flaw of character, some note of history to destroy the credibility of Joseph Smith. . . . His detractors, without exception, . . . have had their day in the sun, and then have faded into oblivion, while the name of Joseph Smith has been honored in ever-widening circles around the earth" ("As One Who Loves the Prophet," 3–4).

In contrast to any flaws his critics have attempted to exploit, an analysis of what Joseph Smith achieved would require volumes. He brought forth the Book of Mormon, another witness and testimony of Jesus Christ; revealed a code of health that has been vindicated in this day of sophisticated medical research; opened our understanding about premortality, the purpose of earth life, and the great plan of happiness; revealed doctrines of the Restoration that are staggering in their import, including the eternal nature of man and the family, and doctrines of salvation for the dead; framed an organization directed by revelation that continues to guide a burgeoning Church; inaugurated an ambitious missionary program that has seen more than one million missionaries serve in this dispensation; built temples and restored temple ordinances; and on and on.

Joseph Smith did all of this without ever having had a

priesthood leader, a bishop or bishop's interview, a Young Men's organization or devoted priesthood advisor, youth conference, EFY or Mutual, or even peers to bolster and spur him onward. He was, however, mentored and sustained by God and His Son, by heavenly messengers, and by family members who believed his account of the Sacred Grove and ever stood by him.

Says President Hinckley, "it is a constantly recurring mystery . . . how some people speak with admiration for the Church and its work while at the same time disdaining him through whom, as a servant of the Lord, came the framework of all that the Church is, of all that it teaches, and of all that it stands for. They would pluck the fruit from the tree while cutting off the root from which it grows" ("Joseph Smith, Jr.— Prophet of God, Mighty Servant," 2).

Key Learnings: Joseph Smith and the Church will always have critics. For each of us, a testimony that Joseph was a prophet is crucial, for if he was the Lord's anointed, then the gospel is true and the Lord's own Church was restored to the earth. If he wasn't a prophet, then the gospel is simply a wise way to live. The Lord counseled the Saints of our dispensation: "Therefore be diligent; stand by my servant Joseph, faithfully, in whatsoever difficult circumstances he may be for the word's sake" (D&C 6:18). Likewise, may we stand not only by Joseph but by his successors, even the living prophets of our day.

9. *The Lord tutors us line upon line, and He knows the end from the begininng.*

Moroni told Joseph that the plates contained "the fulness of the everlasting Gospel" (JS–H 1:34). As ancient records were being prepared, the Lord knew what would become of them, how they would be used, and what they must therefore contain.

Even the Prophet Joseph learned the gospel line upon line. Said Brigham Young: "[Joseph Smith] received the Aaronic Priesthood, and then he received the keys of the Melchisedek Priesthood, and organized the Church. He first received the power to baptise, and still did not know . . . there was more for him. Then he received the keys of the Melchisedek Priesthood, and had power to confirm after he had baptized, which he had not before. He would have stood precisely as John the Baptist stood, had not the Lord sent his other messengers, Peter, James and John, to ordain Joseph to the Melchisedek Priesthood" (*Journal of Discourses*, 18:240). The Lord acknowledged this pattern when he told Joseph, "Ye cannot bear all things now; nevertheless, be of good cheer, for I will lead you along. The kingdom is yours and the blessings thereof are yours, and the riches of eternity are yours" (D&C 78:18).

One insight leads to another, and the more we diligently seek, the more we can expect to uncover the spiritual treasures and wonders of eternity.

Key Learnings: We learn line upon line, precept upon precept. The Lord knows what we need to learn and has prepared messengers, leaders, teachers, parents, and others to help us along the way. One insight leads to another, and the more we diligently seek, the more we can expect to uncover the spiritual treasures and wonders of eternity.

10. There is no limit or end to the influence of a righteous man or woman who has a testimony of Jesus Christ, the Prophet Joseph Smith, and the restoration of the gospel.

John Taylor, who witnessed Joseph and Hyrum seal their testimonies with their lives, declared that "Joseph Smith, the Prophet and Seer of the Lord, has done more, save Jesus only, for the salvation of men in this world, than any other man that ever lived in it. . . . He lived great, and he died great in the eyes of God and his people; and like most of the Lord's anointed in ancient times, has sealed his mission and his works with his own blood; and so has his brother Hyrum. In life they were not divided, and in death they were not separated" (D&C 135:3).

Joseph proved to be, by every measure, "a disturber and an annoyer" of the adversary's kingdom (JS–H 1:20). And so it is with every one of us. We are in a position, every day, to build in ways large and small the kingdom of God, and to join Brother Joseph as latter-day disturbers and annoyers of Lucifer and his minions.

Let us not fall prey to the danger warned of by Brigham Young, that "the sin that will cleave to all the posterity of Adam and Eve is, that they have not done as well as they knew how" (*Discourses of Brigham Young*, 89). As followers of Jesus Christ, and as those who love the Prophet Joseph and who sustain the living prophet, may we express our gratitude for those who brought forth the Restoration by seeking diligently to understand and qualify for access to the power of the Lord.

That power is available to us only because of the Restoration, accomplished through Joseph Smith, whose life testifies that the heavens are open and that God does indeed want a powerful people.

God wants a powerful people, and the most compelling evidence of this fact is that the priesthood has been restored to the earth, and that every one of us—man and woman alike—are the beneficiaries.

CHAPTER EIGHT

THE BLESSINGS OF THE HOLY PRIESTHOOD

I have a deep reverence for the power of the priesthood, and always have. It began with my father. Even as a girl, I sensed there was something magnificent, even holy, about this power because I could feel something when my father blessed me that I felt at no other time. I still vividly remember the Sunday I was confirmed a member of the Church. The confirmation took place during sacrament meeting in the Odd Fellows Hall where our little branch met. Typically, Grandma and I went early to the musty building to sweep up cigarette butts and throw away beer cans left by Saturday night party-goers, and to air out the stale hall to make it more presentable for church. Suffice it to say, the atmosphere didn't lend itself to worship.

In retrospect, that fact makes what I experienced during my confirmation all the more memorable. My father began by con-firming me a member of the Church. When he said the words,

"Receive the Holy Ghost," the Spirit came with such intensity that I began to weep and could not stop. I wept throughout the confirmation and still had a stream running down my face as I went back to my metal folding chair. The waves of emotion didn't stop until the meeting ended. It was only later that I realized I'd been feeling a sustained witness of the Spirit, something that couldn't have happened if it weren't for priesthood power that made that ordinance possible. Though I'd been embarrassed as an eight-year-old by my lack of emotional control, I loved the feeling I had during that ordinance as well as during many priesthood blessings that followed.

My father, as a worthy bearer of the priesthood, was an agent of the Lord who drew upon the very power of God to bless me, baptize and confirm me, heal and comfort and strengthen me.

In simple ways, my father taught me respect, even reverence, for the holy priesthood. As just one example, through all these years, I've never heard him give a blessing in which he didn't say the words, "I do this through no individual power of my own but through the power of the holy Melchizedek Priesthood, which I hold, and in the name of Jesus Christ." As a girl, I heard that phrase over and over again. The repetition planted in my mind and heart the reality that my father, as a worthy bearer of the priesthood, was an agent of the Lord who drew upon the very power of God to bless me, baptize and confirm me, heal and comfort and strengthen me. That phrase somehow underscored for me the divinity and power of the priesthood of God.

As a woman, I don't know that there is anything more inspiring than being in the presence of men who honor and respect the priesthood with which they've been ordained, or more reassuring than receiving a blessing from one who has not only been ordained but has sought to understand that priesthood and prepared himself to exercise it. Said President Boyd K. Packer: "Priesthood is the authority and the power which God has granted to men on earth to act for Him. *When we exercise priesthood authority properly*, we do what He would do if He were present" ("What Every Elder Should Know," 7; emphasis added). And Brigham Young elaborated on what leads to exercising priesthood authority properly when he said, "Men who are vessels of the holy Priesthood . . . should strive continually in their words and actions and daily deportment to do honor to the great dignity of their calling and office as . . . representatives of the Most High" (*Discourses of Brigham Young*, 130).

What could possibly be more comforting to a woman or a man than having the privilege of being blessed by priesthood bearers who exercise priesthood authority righteously? On the other hand, the opposite is also true. It can be spiritually wounding to receive a blessing from someone who is not prepared, for the Spirit withdraws.

The presence of the Spirit when priesthood power is exercised in righteousness, however, is sweet and sustaining. I think of a couple who have been dear friends since our college days. I know something about their efforts to purify themselves and make their lives and their marriage increasingly holy. I know something of this man's persistent seeking to learn how to part the heavens and call upon the power of God, and his willingness to respond when needed, even at great inconvenience to himself. Because I haven't yet had the privilege of marrying and therefore having a priesthood bearer in my home, my friend has often been the "older brother" to whom I have turned in times of need for blessings. I have been the beneficiary of his preparation as he has petitioned the Lord in my behalf and pronounced blessings that are always accompanied by a confirmation of the Spirit.

Being ordained to hold the priesthood is a holy and sacred privilege as well as a grand and imposing responsibility. It is an opportunity to draw directly upon the power of God, to speak in His name, to bless as He would bless. It is, therefore, the privilege of serving in a way unique among all mankind. Said Elder Bruce R. McConkie, "Be it noted, every holder of the priesthood has a calling to minister, in one way or another, to the inhabitants of the earth" (A New Witness for the Articles of Faith, 310).

President Hinckley has spoken strongly about the obligations of those ordained to the priesthood: "Our behavior in public must be above reproach. Our behavior in private is even more important. It must clear the standard set by the Lord. We cannot indulge in sin, let alone try to cover our sins. We cannot gratify our pride. We cannot partake of the vanity of unrighteous ambition. We cannot exercise control, or dominion, or compulsion upon our wives or children, or any others in any degree of unrighteousness. If we do any of these things, the powers of heaven are withdrawn. The Spirit of the Lord is grieved. The very virtue of our priesthood is nullified. Its authority is lost. . . . [The priesthood] is not as a cloak that we put on and take off at will. It is, when exercised in righteousness, as the very tissue of our bodies, a part of us at all times and in all circumstances. . . . There is nothing else to compare with it in all this world. Safeguard it, cherish it, love it, live worthy of it" ("Personal Worthiness to Exercise the Priesthood," 52, 59).

A man is never more magnificent, nor is he ever more like the Savior, than when he is honoring and acting within the bounds of the priesthood he holds, and when it is clear that he has sought to understand how to exercise that power.

For, as revealed through the Prophet Joseph, "The rights of the priesthood are inseparably connected with the powers of heaven, and . . . the powers of heaven cannot be controlled nor handled only upon the principles of righteousness. That they may be conferred upon us, it is true; but when we undertake to cover our sins, or to gratify our pride, our vain ambition, or to

A man is never more magnificent than when he is honoring and acting within the bounds of the priesthood he holds, and when it is clear that he has sought to understand how to exercise that power.

exercise control or dominion or compulsion upon the souls of the children of men, in any degree of unrighteousness, behold, the heavens withdraw themselves; the Spirit of the Lord is grieved; and when it is withdrawn, Amen to the priesthood or the authority of that man" (D&C 121:36–37).

Just as foreordination is not enough, as mentioned in an earlier chapter, ordination isn't enough either. Ordination is but the beginning, for a man must learn how to use the power with which he has been ordained. That requires study, seeking, prayer, purity, and growing in the priesthood. As a woman who has been blessed many times by worthy priesthood bearers who have paid the price to live up to their ordination, I am profoundly grateful to and for them.

Likewise, I have had the privilege of serving under the direction of inspired priesthood leaders at all levels of Church government. It is the Lord who determined that men would be ordained to the priesthood while women would not, though they both would receive equally compelling and crucial assignments. Women are not assigned to direct the ecclesiastical affairs of the Church. Men are. Women are not required or eligible to be ordained. Men are. Women are not required to hold the priesthood in order to enter the House of the Lord. Men are. The Lord has not elaborated on His rationale about these matters, He has only declared His will. I happily accept His pattern for the governance of His Church as pure doctrine, knowing that it is inconsistent with the character of God that He could love, cherish, or favor His sons more than His daughters, or His daughters more than His sons.

Nonetheless, I realize there are those who are unsettled about the Lord's pattern for men and women. Through the years, I have been approached by women troubled by the fact that they are not eligible for priesthood ordination because they construe that to mean they are lesser-class citizens in the kingdom of God. I have never felt this way—in part because of my upbringing, but also because I have studied, pondered, and prayed about these issues over many years. And as I have sought knowledge in the temple about priesthood power and its relationship to both men and women, as well as the division of responsibilities between men and women, my reverence and gratitude for priesthood power, the power of God delegated to man on earth, has only increased and intensified. God wants a powerful people, and the most compelling evidence of this fact is that the priesthood has been restored to the earth, and that every one of us—man and woman alike—are the beneficiaries.

Women do not have the responsibility of officiating in the ordinances of the priesthood and directing the ecclesiastical affairs of the Church. In turn, men do not have the privilege or responsibility of bringing spirit sons and daughters into mortality and taking a leading role in their nurture. Clearly, the Lord established a division of responsibility between women and men that in His wisdom allows maximum potential for the growth, development, and nurturing of His children as well as His kingdom, both on a grand scale as well as one-on-one.

The answers to questions related to priesthood, manhood, motherhood, and womanhood are in the temple. They are in the scriptures. They are in the teachings of latter-day prophets and Apostles. And, most significantly, they are in the whisperings of the Spirit. All of these make it clear that, while ordination to the priesthood is not available to or necessary for women, priesthood power and access to that power is both available and necessary for all worthy members of the Church.

The fruits of priesthood power are for everyone. Uncategorically. Undeniably. And without restrictions to those who qualify.

One reason some may feel unsettled in their feelings about the priesthood is that we sometimes confuse the privilege of holding the priesthood with the blessings of the priesthood.

One reason some may feel unsettled in their feelings about the priesthood is that we sometimes confuse the privilege of *holding* the priesthood with the *blessings* of the priesthood. We sometimes confuse the blessings of priesthood power with ordination to the priesthood.

The blessings and fruits that derive from the priesthood are greater than those concerned with holding the priesthood, though the blessing of ordination cannot be overstated, for it allows a man to serve others in the way God would and does. Nonetheless, the terms *priesthood power* and *priesthood bearers* are often used interchangeably—which can lead to misunderstanding.

At a recent stake Relief Society women's conference, the stake president concluded the meeting, "I now wish to bless the women of this stake, and particularly those of you who don't have the priesthood in your home." It would have been more helpful and accurate if he had said, "and particularly those of you who don't have a priesthood bearer in your home."

Not long ago I attended a Relief Society class where the instructor, a wise woman seasoned in the gospel by decades of study and service, taught a lesson about the priesthood. Her entire focus was on "supporting the priesthood"—meaning, priesthood bearers—and expressing gratitude for "having the priesthood in her home"—meaning, a husband who was a priesthood bearer. Although these ideas are important, there was an unfortunate vacuum, as there was no discussion of the blessings derived from the priesthood—what it is and does, what it enables us to receive, and how it affects all members of the Church. It was a missed opportunity to teach the doctrine of the priesthood.

Elder Bruce R. McConkie explained why some of these deficiencies and inaccuracies slip into our teaching: "[The] doctrine of the priesthood—unknown in the world and *but little known even in the Church*—cannot be learned out of the scriptures alone. . . . *The doctrine of the priesthood is known only by personal revelation.* It comes, line upon line and precept upon precept, by the power of the Holy Ghost to those who love and serve God with all their heart, might, mind, and strength" ("The Doctrine of the Priesthood," 32; emphasis added).

Elder McConkie's declaration is enlightening. In delegating His power to men on earth, God has made the fruits of that power available to righteous, believing, faithful sons and daughters. But it is consistent with His pattern for teaching His children that He would reveal, line upon line, the depth and breadth of His own power only to those who cherish it, live worthy of that knowledge, and seek to know how to draw upon and exercise that power. How critical it is, then, that we search holy writ and the words of prophets, and seek personal revelation to better understand what God has given us.

To this end, may I share a number of statements from Church leaders that are integral to an understanding of the doctrine of the priesthood. As you read these statements, you may wish to ponder some basic questions: What difference do these doctrines make in *your* life? Do these doctrines enhance or change the way you see yourself, your gender, your marriage and family, your stewardship, your purpose, your potential, the doctrine of priesthood, or your access to the blessings of the priesthood?

1. The Prophet Joseph Smith taught that "the Melchizedek Priesthood . . . is the grand head, and holds the highest authority which pertains to the priesthood, and the keys of the Kingdom of God in all ages of the world to the latest posterity on the earth; and is the channel through which all knowledge, doctrine, the plan of salvation and every important matter is revealed from heaven. . . . It is the channel through which the Almighty commenced revealing His glory at the beginning of the creation of this earth, and through which He has continued to reveal Himself to the children of men to the present time, and through which He will make known His purposes to the end of time" (*Teachings*, 166–67).

2. President John Taylor defined priesthood power in this

comprehensive way: "What is priesthood? . . . It is the government of God, whether on the earth or in the heavens, for it is by that power, agency, or principle that all things are governed on the earth and in the heavens, and by that power that all things are upheld and sustained. It governs all things—it directs all things—it sustains all things—and has to do with all things that God and truth are associated with. It is the power of God delegated to intelligences in the heavens and to men on the earth" (*The Gospel Kingdom*, 129).

3. President Joseph Fielding Smith taught: "There is no exaltation in the kingdom of God without the fullness of the priesthood, and every man who receives the Melchizedek Priesthood does so with an oath and a covenant that he shall be exalted. . . . [But] the blessings of the priesthood are not confined to men alone. These blessings are also poured out upon . . . all the faithful women of the Church. . . . The Lord offers to his daughters every spiritual gift and blessing that can be obtained by his sons" ("Magnifying Our Callings in the Priesthood," 66).

4. Again, from President Joseph Fielding Smith: "It ought to make every man among us who holds the priesthood rejoice to think that we have that great authority by which we may know God. Not only the men holding the priesthood know that great truth, but because of that priesthood and the ordinances thereof, every member of the Church, men and women alike, may know God" (*Doctrines of Salvation*, 3:142–43).

5. President Joseph Fielding Smith further taught: "If you want salvation in its fullest, that is exaltation in the kingdom

of God, so that you may become his sons and his daughters, you have got to go into the temple. . . . No man shall receive . . . that blessing alone; but man and wife, when they receive the sealing power in the temple of the Lord, shall pass on to exaltation, and shall continue and become like the Lord" (*Elijah: The Prophet and His Mission*, 24).

6. The significance of entering the new and everlasting covenant of marriage is unmistakable, for that order of the priesthood is filled with power. Indeed, at a sealing I attended not long ago, the sealer began by telling the couple being married that when he was given the sealing power, he was told that this was neither a calling nor an office, but a transferral of power. Joseph Smith said that "The power of the Melchizedek Priesthood is to have the power of 'endless lives'" (*Teachings*, 322). Elder Bruce R. McConkie explained further: "Endless lives are eternal lives; they are a continuation of the lives or a continuation of the seeds; they are spirit children in the resurrection. The blessing of so obtaining comes to those who receive the fulness of the priesthood; they become, thus, inheritors of eternal life through the continuation of the family unit in eternity. . . . The Lord says that 'the fulness of the priesthood' is received only in the temple itself " (*A New Witness for the Articles of Faith*, 314–15).

Through the Prophet Joseph Smith, the Lord revealed that there are three degrees in the celestial glory, "And in order to obtain the highest, a man must enter into this order of the priesthood [meaning the new and everlasting covenant of marriage]; And if he does not, he cannot obtain it" (D&C

131:1–3). Further, the Prophet revealed that those who keep the commandments sufficiently well, except the law of celestial marriage, having had opportunity but rejecting it, "cannot be enlarged, but remain separately and singly, without exaltation, . . . to all eternity; and from henceforth are not gods" (D&C 132:17).

Simply stated, when a man or woman is endowed in the House of the Lord, he or she is "endowed with power from on high" (D&C 38:32), which by definition is the Lord's power. Further, when a man and woman enter the new and everlasting covenant of marriage, they enter an order of the priesthood, which order can be entered into *only* by a righteous man and a righteous woman *together*. This truth alone has profound implications for both women and men.

7. Elder James E. Talmage said: "It is not given to women to exercise the authority of the Priesthood independently; nevertheless, in the sacred endowments associated with the ordinances pertaining to the House of the Lord, woman shares with man the blessings of the Priesthood. . . . In the glorified state of the blessed hereafter, husband and wife will administer in their respective stations, seeing and understanding alike, and co-operating to the full in the government of their family kingdom. . . . Then shall woman reign by Divine right, a queen in the resplendent realm of her glorified state, even as exalted man shall stand, priest and king unto the Most High God. Mortal eye cannot see nor mind comprehend the beauty, glory, and majesty of a righteous woman made perfect in the celestial kingdom of God" ("The Eternity of Sex," 602–3).

8. Elder Talmage also taught: "Women of the Church share the authority of the Priesthood with their husbands, actual or prospective; and therefore women . . . are not ordained to specific rank in the Priesthood. Nevertheless there is no grade, rank, or phase of the temple endowment to which women are not eligible on an equality with men. . . . The married state is regarded as sacred, sanctified, and holy in all temple procedure; and within the House of the Lord the woman is the equal and the help-meet of the man. In the privileges and blessings of that holy place, the utterance of Paul is regarded as a scriptural decree in full force and effect: 'Neither is the man without the woman, neither the woman without the man, in the Lord.'" (*House of the Lord*, 79).

9. Elder John A. Widtsoe explained priesthood as it relates to men and women in this way: "The Priesthood is for the benefit of all members of the Church. Men have no greater claim than women upon the blessings that issue from the Priesthood and accompany its possession. Woman does not hold the Priesthood, but she is a partaker of the blessings of the Priesthood. That is, the man holds the Priesthood, performs the priestly duties of the Church, but his wife enjoys with him every other privilege derived from the possession of the Priesthood. This is made clear, as an example, in the Temple. . . . The ordinances of the Temple are distinctly of Priesthood character, yet women have access to all of them, and the highest blessings of the Temple are conferred only upon a man and wife jointly" (*Priesthood and Church Government*, 83).

10. And again from Elder Widtsoe: "In the Church there is

full equality between man and woman. . . . The Lord loves His daughters as well as He loves His sons. This doctrine of equality is confirmed in the ordinances of the Church which are alike for man and woman. Faith, repentance, baptism are the same for all. The rewards, such as the gift of the Holy Ghost, and the temple ordinances, are alike. The highest attainable glory cannot be won by man or woman alone. Only those who are united, as husband and wife, by the sealing power, can attain exaltation in the celestial glory in the hereafter. . . . There can be no question in the Church of man's rights versus woman's rights. They have the same and equal rights" (*Evidences and Reconciliations*, 305).

11. President J. Reuben Clark Jr. taught: "To provide mortal bodies and a mortal life and experience for the waiting spirits, was the very purpose of the creation. Adam, still in intimate association with the Lord, must have remembered at least a part of what he knew before he was made . . . , and, if so, he must have recalled the eternal truth of motherhood. . . . Notwithstanding the great powers of the Priesthood which he held, Adam was powerless to go forward by himself, to the providing of earthly tabernacles for the spirits eager to enter into their 'second estate.' . . . To work all this out, it was indispensable that the Priesthood, powerful as it was, must have help. Adam must have an helpmeet. . . . So came Eve, an helpmeet to the Priesthood mission of Adam—Eve the last created being in the creation of the world, without whom the whole creation of the world . . . would have been in vain and the purposes of God have come to naught. . . . This is the place of our wives

and of our mothers in the Eternal Plan. They are not bearers of the Priesthood; they are not charged with carrying out the duties and functions of the Priesthood; nor are they laden with its responsibilities; they are builders and organizers under its power, and partakers of its blessings, possessing the complement of the Priesthood powers and possessing a function as divinely called, as eternally important in its place as the Priesthood itself" ("Our Wives and Our Mothers in the Eternal Plan," 799–801).

12. More recently, President Spencer W. Kimball taught that the roles and assignments of men and women differ, with "women being given many tremendous responsibilities of motherhood and sisterhood and men being given the tremendous responsibilities of fatherhood and the priesthood. . . . Remember, in the world before we came here, faithful women were given certain assignments while faithful men were fore-ordained to certain priesthood tasks. While we do not now remember the particulars, this does not alter the glorious reality of what we once agreed to" ("Role of Righteous Women," 102).

13. In 1995 the First Presidency and Council of the Twelve declared in "The Family: A Proclamation to the World," that "marriage is essential to [God's] eternal plan. . . . By divine design, fathers are to preside over their families in love and righteousness and are responsible to provide the necessities of life and protection for their families. Mothers are primarily responsible for the nurture of their children. In these sacred responsibilities, fathers and mothers are obligated to help one another as equal partners."

Because the priesthood has been restored, all of us are eligible to receive gifts of the Spirit and the gift of the Holy Ghost, personal revelation, and a patriarchal blessing that declares our lineage and gives us guidance for our life's mission. We are all blessed by the revelation that comes to the Church through prophets, seers, and revelators. We may all take upon us the Lord's name, become sons and daughters of Christ, partake of the ordinances of the temple, enter the new and everlasting covenant of marriage, receive the fulness of the gospel and a "fulness of the Holy Ghost" (D&C 109:15), and achieve exaltation in the celestial kingdom—which is available only to men and women who have entered the new and everlasting covenant of marriage and then been faithful to that covenant. These spiritual blessings emanate from the Melchizedek Priesthood, which holds the "keys of all the spiritual blessings of the church" (D&C 107:18).

Men and women alike are magnified, purified, sanctified, strengthened, sealed, ennobled, and ultimately perfected by priesthood power.

It's worth pondering what *all the spiritual blessings of the Church* include in the context of this scripture: "To have the privilege of receiving the mysteries of the kingdom of heaven, to have the heavens opened . . . , to commune with the general assembly and church of the Firstborn, and to enjoy the communion and presence of God the Father, and Jesus the mediator of the new covenant" (D&C 107:19).

Men and women alike are magnified, purified, sanctified, strengthened, sealed, ennobled, and ultimately perfected by priesthood power. In fact, as Elder Widtsoe proclaimed, "The Priesthood when exercised righteously unites men and women; it never separates them, unless either group, by their own acts, cuts off its power" (*Priesthood and Church Government*, 93). This is particularly true for the men and women who have received their endowment, for the endowment is a gift or a bestowal of power and knowledge.

Considering the statements above, those who have been to the temple may wish to consider several questions:

—With what was I endowed or gifted in the House of the Lord? What does that gift mean to me and how may I use it?

—What do I learn there? What do I learn to *do?*

—What do I learn about the power of God versus the power of the adversary?

—What do I learn about communicating with the heavens?

—What does it mean to receive a "fulness of the Holy Ghost" (D&C 109:15) and a fullness of the priesthood?

—When a man and woman enter the new and everlasting covenant of marriage, what kind of power do they share?

Throughout modern revelation, particularly the Doctrine and Covenants, the word *receive* is used to mean "have faith in" or "accept as true." Do not all of us, including those who are not eligible to be ordained, *receive* and therefore activate the blessings of the priesthood in our lives by *believing* the priesthood to be the power of God and having faith in its governance, by *seeking* those blessings and *keeping* sacred covenants, and by *sustaining* those who are ordained and called to lead us?

And do not those ordained to the priesthood receive it in other ways? Said President Spencer W. Kimball: "The Lord has made clear that they who receive his priesthood receive him. And I think that means more than just sitting in a chair and having somebody put his hands upon your head. I think when you receive it, you accept it. You do not just merely sit. 'And he that receiveth my Father receiveth my Father's kingdom; therefore all that my Father hath shall be given unto him.' Can you imagine anything greater? Shouldn't we be frightened, almost awed as we contemplate the honor we have and the responsibility we have that has come from the oath and the covenant?" (in Stockholm Sweden Area Conference Report, 1974, 100).

> *Are we receiving the privileges and unspeakable blessings associated with the gift of priesthood power?*

Brigham Young taught that "the Priesthood is given to the people . . . and, when properly understood, they may actually unlock the treasury of the Lord, and *receive* to their fullest satisfaction" (*Discourses of Brigham Young*, 131; emphasis added).

Surely the "treasury of the Lord" includes the "wonders of eternity" (D&C 76:8) and the "riches of eternity" (D&C 38:39) the Lord wishes to give us. It is the power of the priesthood that unlocks the door to heaven and allows us to understand, one by one and line upon line, the mysteries of

God—or how God works. The question we might properly ask ourselves is, Are we receiving the privileges and unspeakable blessings associated with the gift of priesthood power by believing, seeking, and sustaining for women, and by being ordained and living worthy of that ordination for men? And are we rejoicing in Him who gave us this priceless gift?

In the October 1977 general conference, Elder Bruce R. McConkie spoke about the "ten blessings of the priesthood." Note that men and women, married and unmarried, can enjoy almost all of these blessings by virtue of their Church membership. The blessings Elder McConkie outlined are as followed:

First, being members of the Church and receiving the fulness of the gospel.

Second, receiving the gift of the Holy Ghost and other gifts of the Spirit.

Third, being sanctified by the Spirit.

Fourth, representing Jesus Christ in administering salvation to mankind.

Fifth, becoming children of God in the family of the Lord Jesus Christ.

Sixth, entering the new and everlasting covenant of marriage, without which there is no exaltation in the highest degree of the celestial kingdom.

Seventh, having the power to govern all temporal and spiritual things.

Eighth, having the power to gain eternal life.

Ninth, having power to make one's calling and election sure while in mortality.

Tenth, having the power and privilege to see the face of God in mortality (see "The Ten Blessings of the Priesthood, 33–35).

In the rancorous era in which we live, some will try to convince Latter-day Saint women that because they are not ordained to hold the priesthood, they have been shortchanged, and Latter-day Saint men that women are second-class citizens in the kingdom of God. Those who believe these and other lies about men and women in the gospel kingdom are either uninformed, flat-out wrong, or deceived, for they do not understand the doctrines of the gospel of Jesus Christ. They do not understand how our Father feels about and regards both His daughters and His sons. They do not understand the respect Jesus Christ demonstrated for women during His mortality. It was Mary Magdalene to whom the Savior first revealed Himself after His Resurrection. It was Mary Magadalene whom He instructed to tell His disciples that He had risen (see John 20:1–18). Perhaps this episode, as much as any other, reflects how the Father and the Son feel about women and their place in the kingdom of God.

Further, there are those who do not understand the confidence the Savior has placed in men as watchmen on the tower and administrators of His kingdom.

Satan understands the power of the priesthood and devotes his considerable power to undermining it, "hiding" its power from view, confusing women about how the priesthood affects them, distracting ordained men from seeking to understand their ordination, and, through it all, discouraging men and women from uniting in righteousness. He is still stinging from his banishment into eternal exile after Michael led the hosts of heaven, comprised of valiant men and women united in the cause of Christ, against him. Lucifer seems particularly determined to devour marriages and families, because their demise threatens to destabilize not only mortal society but the salvation of all involved and the vitality of the Lord's kingdom itself. Thus, from time immemorial Satan has attempted to confuse us about our stewardships and to blur distinct messages about gender, marriage, family, male-female relationships, and priesthood power.

Not only is the power of the priesthood the greatest power in heaven and on earth, but it is the one power in mortality that can only be used righteously.

Our Father knew exactly what He was doing when He created us as men and women. He made us enough alike to love, value, and be attracted to each other, but enough different that we would complement each other and would in fact need to unite our strengths and weaknesses to create a whole. Neither man nor woman is perfect or complete without the other. Thus, no marriage or family, no ward or stake is likely to reach its full potential until husbands and wives, mothers and fathers, men and women work together in unity of purpose, respecting and relying upon each other's strengths.

Within the priesthood is great power: the power to

separate and safeguard us from the world, the power to subdue the adversary and surmount obstacles, the power to comfort, bless, and heal, the power to enlarge our physical and spiritual capacity and enable us to hear the voice of the Lord, the power to strengthen marriages and families and bind us to each other, and the power to triumph over mortality and come unto Him. These blessings may be received by every righteous, seeking son or daughter.

Not only is the power of the priesthood the greatest power in heaven and on earth, but it is the one power in mortality that can only be used righteously. Further, priesthood power can only be used according to the will of God. President Spencer W. Kimball taught a significant truth in this regard: "The power of the priesthood is limitless but God has wisely placed upon each of us certain limitations. I may develop priesthood power as I perfect my life, yet I am grateful that even through the priesthood I cannot heal all the sick. I might heal people who should die. I might relieve people of suffering who should suffer. I fear I would frustrate the purposes of God. Had I limitless power, and yet limited vision and understanding, . . . I fear that had I been in Carthage Jail on June 27, 1844, I might have deflected the bullets that pierced the body of the Prophet and the Patriarch. I might have saved them from the sufferings and agony, but lost to them the martyr's death and reward. I am glad I did not have to make that decision. . . . I would not dare to take the responsibility of bringing back to life my loved ones. Christ himself acknowledged the difference between his will and the Father's when he prayed that the cup of suffering be taken from him; yet he added,

'Nevertheless, not my will but thine be done'" (*Faith Precedes the Miracle*, 99–100).

Thus, priesthood—which is a power like none other on earth, the very power of God Himself, the power that governs heaven and earth and by which the worlds were made—is without end, but its use is governed by the faith of those involved and by the will of God.

This glorious power by which all things are governed, preserved, protected, and upheld will be a vital source of strength and protection in our families and throughout the Church in the days ahead, for it is the priesthood of God that distinguishes the Lord's church from any other. Wherever and whenever its power and blessings are exercised, we may expect to find peace, security, direction, and protection.

While serving in the Relief Society general presidency, I traveled one weekend to an assignment in Colorado. As I boarded the plane on Friday afternoon for Colorado Springs, I was exhausted. The week had been unusually grueling, and I was so tired that I dreaded the weekend ahead of me. I napped on the quick flight but still felt groggy as I landed, greeted family living in the area, and headed to the stake center.

The chapel and cultural hall were filled to overflowing with a magnificent gathering of Relief Society sisters. Because of the sweet and sustaining spirit they brought with them, the Spirit came in abundance, and by meeting's end, I felt rejuvenated—enough that I decided to make the two-hour drive that night to Ft. Collins, where I was assigned to speak early the next morning. I thought that, if anything, the drive through the Denver metroplex would go more quickly on a late Friday evening than during the day.

Much to my chagrin, however, about halfway through Denver, traffic came to a standstill. A tanker had rolled over, and the freeway was shut down. By that time, my fatigue had returned, only worse. To stay awake, I called and woke up a dear friend, who talked to me until I finally reached Ft. Collins—three hours later—at 2:00 A.M.

After four hours of sleep, I awoke feeling emotionally, spiritually, and physically depleted—so tired that as I knelt to pray, I began to cry. I pleaded with the Lord for help, mentioning that the only way I could imagine speaking to another stake center full of sisters, then driving six hours south to speak again that night, was if I could receive a priesthood blessing. I concluded my prayer, knowing I had no choice but to get ready and drive to the stake center.

Waiting for me as I walked in the door was the presiding stake president, who greeted me and said, "Sister Dew, we hadn't planned on having a prayer meeting, but I think it would be well if we had a prayer together. I've invited our stake Relief Society presidency to join us." At that point, this great stake president, whom I had met just moments before, began to pray. And his was not a predictable "bless-the-meeting" kind of prayer. In fact, his prayer was all about me. He prayed in a familiar manner that I would be guided by the Spirit, but then asked that I be physically invigorated, that I have the strength to do all required of me that day, and that I be blessed with safety and protection. He didn't have his hands on my head,

163

but it felt as though I was receiving a priesthood blessing. The Spirit in the room was undeniable.

After the stake president finished, I motioned for the others to walk out ahead of me so that I could say something to this remarkable priesthood leader. "You couldn't have known, President, but this morning I—"

At that point, he interrupted me, "Actually, Sister Dew, I did know that you were in need of a blessing, and I felt this might be the best way to accomplish that."

That day, the Lord knew who I was, where I was, what my mission was, and what I needed to accomplish that mission. The Lord blessed me—figuratively and literally—through a priesthood leader in tune with the Spirit whose keys enabled him to enable me to fulfill my assignment.

I contrast that experience with another Relief Society training assignment. For some reason, no presiding officer had been assigned to the meeting in question. Though there were many priesthood leaders present, no one had been assigned to preside. That evening was a disaster. If I had been standing on the rim

When women understand and fully respect the fact that the Church is governed by the power of the priesthood, and when priesthood leaders in turn acknowledge the vital contribution of women, the Lord's work can move forward to bless countless people.

of the Grand Canyon preaching to the wildlife at the bottom of that impressive gorge, I would have been more effective than I was that night. The circumstances were not right. They did not follow God's order. Brigham Young explained why: "There is no act of a Latter-day Saint—no duty required—no time given, exclusive and independent of the Priesthood. Everything is subject to it, whether preaching, business, or any other act" (*Discourses of Brigham Young*, 133). Though I attempted to teach virtually the same material I always taught, my ability, even my power, to reach those Saints was stripped by the absence of a presiding officer. It was a powerful lesson in Church government, order, and priesthood power.

When women understand and fully respect the fact that the Church is governed by the power of the priesthood, and when priesthood leaders in turn acknowledge the vital contribution of women, the Lord's work can move forward to bless countless people. This can happen in every ward and stake and, first and foremost, in every home as we learn to rejoice in each other's unique gifts and strengths and as we gratefully rejoice in the pattern the Lord has established for the governance, protection, and power of His people. Blessings will flow as we acknowledge by our obedience and faith that the priesthood is the power of God to bless and exalt every one of us, if we live worthy of and seek its blessings.

There may be few things we can do of greater importance than persistently seeking to understand, line upon line, what the Lord gave us when He restored His power to the earth. For that gift, that act, is the greatest evidence of all that God does indeed want a powerful people.

In this great latter-day battle, the Lord needs every True Follower to step forward—in every part of His kingdom—to draw upon and use every gift and endowment we've been given. There isn't a week, a day, an hour to lose.

CHAPTER NINE

TRUE FOLLOWERS

One weekend not long ago a commitment took me to
Albany, New York. Because I needed to be back in
Salt Lake City by Saturday evening, I arranged to
complete my assignment by midafternoon so I could catch a
quick, thirty-five-minute commuter flight to JFK International
Airport in New York City, and then a direct flight home.

All went as planned, and when I checked in at the Albany
airport, my flight to JFK was showing on time—though the air-
craft we were to board hadn't yet arrived in Albany. That was
when things started to get interesting. First the gate agent
announced there would be a fifteen-minute delay. No worries;
I had ninety minutes to connect at JFK. Then she announced
there would be a forty-five-minute delay because the plane we
were taking to JFK had not yet *left* JFK to come to Albany. I
started getting antsy. Forty-five minutes to make a connection
in JFK was enough, but barely. That airport is huge and *always*

a mass of confusion (not to mention under construction). It has sometimes been likened to the Bermuda Triangle—you can get in, but you can't get out. I had specifically booked an earlier-than-needed flight out of Albany precisely because JFK can be, well, a pain to connect through.

I approached the gate agent, asked if there were any other way to get back to Salt Lake City that night, and learned there was one way—but it would require connections in three cities and basically had the look and feel of a milk run. I weighed the odds of gambling that three flights would be on time and connect as scheduled, or still making the connection at JFK, and decided to stick with the JFK connection—even though our plane still had not arrived.

Every minute started to feel like twenty, and then the gate agent made the fateful announcement: Our flight was going to be delayed at least an hour and fifteen minutes. Ugh! By now, it was too late to attempt the other routing. I was stuck. I couldn't see any way I could get home that evening, and started phoning to cancel commitments.

Finally our plane arrived and we took off for JFK, more than seventy-five minutes late. By the time we landed and taxied to the spot on the tarmac where this little commuter plane parked (it wasn't large enough to pull up to the concourse), I had eight minutes before my flight to Salt Lake was to leave.

By the time they finally let us off the plane—we had to wait for the propellers to stop spinning—I had four minutes to make my connection. And I wasn't yet even inside the terminal! But even though I *knew* I wouldn't make it, I had the impression to at least try. So I grabbed my luggage and began running through the inevitable construction maze to get to the door on the lower level of the concourse. From there I climbed two flights of stairs, finally made my way onto the concourse, and dashed toward my gate, trying very hard not to mow down other passengers in my path.

With no time left I spotted my gate in the distance, could see the gate agent closing the door to the jetway, and called as loudly as I dared, "Don't close that door!" The agent looked up, saw a harried woman racing toward him, started to laugh, and pulled the door back open. "Please tell me I still have a seat on this plane," I nearly begged. He grinned, acting quite the hero in announcing that yes, I still had a seat, took my boarding pass, and ushered me into the jetway. I made the flight.

Now, for the rest of the story. About midway through the five-hour flight home, I suddenly felt a presence at my elbow and realized that a man was kneeling in the aisle next to my seat. He introduced himself and then explained that he and his wife were returning from Europe where, while on vacation, they had learned that his mother-in-law had unexpectedly passed away. "My wife is struggling so much with the sudden loss of her mother," he said, "and particularly with the fact that she wasn't able to say good-bye. Would you be willing to talk with her? I think it would bring her some comfort."

I told him I'd do my best, switched seats with him, and found myself visiting with his lovely but sad wife. We had talked for only a few moments when I suddenly realized we had a great deal in common. My family has suffered several untimely deaths, and I knew what it was to get an emergency phone call in a hotel room in a distant city with the news that someone I loved dearly had suddenly passed away, without warning. We spoke of that, and I shared what I had learned in the process, particularly about the balm of Gilead, the comforting power of the Savior.

Now, to the point. Ask anyone. It is *not possible* to make a connection at JFK in four minutes. And yet I did. It isn't possible that I found myself seated one row in front of a woman who was having an experience similar to several I've had, but I did. (In retrospect, I'm guessing the Lord's intervention in my flight plans that day was entirely about helping that good woman, rather than allowing me to keep my original schedule. The Lord more often works miracles when His doing so enables us to help someone else.)

> *The Lord more often works miracles when His doing so enables us to help someone else.*

Sometimes things aren't possible. And yet, they are.

It wasn't possible that the Father and the Son would appear to a fourteen-year-old farm boy, who was making his first attempt to pray vocally, in a grove of trees in upstate New York. But They did.

It is not possible that a little church organized in a rough-hewn log cabin in Fayette, New York, on April 6, 1830, by a twenty-four-year-old prophet, would one day fill the earth. But it is.

When I was growing up, it wasn't even conceivable that

missionaries would serve behind the Iron Curtain. But today they labor in Russia, the Ukraine, Bulgaria, Romania, Lithuania, Estonia, Hungary, and many other countries where former regimes denied their people freedom of religion.

Even today, with political conflicts around the globe, it is hard to imagine that the gospel will go to every nation, kindred, tongue, and people. But it will. And it is.

It isn't possible to live a pure life in a grungy world. But millions are doing it, including thousands of youth and young adults who are worthy to enter the temple, serve missions as part of what Elder M. Russell Ballard called the "greatest generation of missionaries in the history of the Church" ("The Greatest Generation of Missionaries," 47), and marry in the House of the Lord.

It isn't possible, or at least reasonable, to think we are capable of filling the measure of our creation and passing our probationary test in mortality during the most complex time in the history of the world. But we are. Here we are, sent now because our Father knew in His infinite wisdom that we would have the courage, determination, faith, and pure grit to fulfill successfully and completely our mission in the latter part of the latter days.

And surely it isn't possible for regular people like you and me to talk with God and learn to draw upon His power. But it *is* possible—because with God, nothing is impossible. In fact, it is what our Father desires for His children.

All of these things weren't or aren't possible. And yet they are happening, some of them every day, because God the Father and God the Son are Gods of miracles.

Explaining the miraculous process by which the Book of Mormon would be recorded and preserved for the latter days, God declared, "For behold, I am God; and I am a God of miracles; and I will show unto the world that I am the same yesterday, today, and forever; and I work not among the children of men save it be according to their faith" (2 Nephi 27:23).

It is difficult, actually impossible, for our mortal minds to comprehend what it really means to know that the Father of our spirits is God, even Elohim, who has no limit to His majesty, His dominion, His glory, His righteousness, His wisdom, or His power. We are His spirit children. He wants us to become as He is.

Thus the necessity for us to experience mortality, a period of probation, to see if we will do what we've been sent here to do. We are here to fulfill the measure of our creation and the wonderful missions for which we've been sent to earth. We are here to determine by our actions if we want to be part of the kingdom of God more than we want anything else.

The only way anyone can accomplish all he or she is intended to do is to become a True Follower of Jesus Christ—a True Follower who qualifies to draw upon His power, and learns how to do so.

As discussed earlier, the Atonement is filled with power— redemptive, enabling, sanctifying, strengthening, healing power. A verse in Mormon's classic discourse on faith, hope, and charity teaches us *how* to draw upon that power. We are to "pray unto the Father with all the energy of heart," meaning the kind of energy we expend when we are desperate for help, peace, or solace, that we may be "filled with this love, which he [meaning our Father] hath *bestowed* [meaning it is a gift] upon all who are *true followers* of his Son, Jesus Christ (Moroni 7:48; emphasis added).

Every gift we seek from our Father is a bestowal. For "every good gift and every perfect gift is from above, and cometh down from the Father of lights" (James 1:17). We don't earn these gifts. They are just that: Gifts. Bestowals. Endowments. We can, however, qualify for them.

Eternal life is "the greatest of all the gifts of God" (D&C 14:7).

Perfection will ultimately be a gift from God. We may qualify for it, but we won't earn it.

Perfection will ultimately be a gift from God. We may qualify for it, but we won't earn it.

Testimony is a gift. For "to some it is given by the Holy Ghost to know that Jesus Christ is the Son of God" (D&C 46:13).

Peace is a gift. Hope is a gift. Charity, the pure love of Christ, the very essence of who the Father and Son are, is a gift. Knowledge, particularly knowledge of the mysteries of godliness, is a gift.

Deliverance is a gift—deliverance from pain or weakness, deliverance from tribulation, deliverance from sin, deliverance from whatever is holding us back or down. It is given to all those whom the Lord has chosen, because of their faith in

Christ, "to make them mighty even unto the power of deliverance" (1 Nephi 1:20; see also Alma 14:26).

Every kind of divine healing is a gift. The Lord has promised to heal our broken hearts (Luke 4:18), to heal our infirmities and afflictions (Alma 7:11–12), to heal our wounded souls (Jacob 2:8), to heal our imperfect personalities and emotions and spiritual wounds, to heal our natural-man, natural-woman selves (Mosiah 3:19), to heal us from the effects of sin when we repent, to heal us by delivering us from whatever and whoever has held us captive.

These gifts are bestowals from our Father. Moroni exhorted us to "lay hold upon every good gift" (Moroni 10:30). And they are gifts available to True Followers of the Son. For, as Elder Bruce R. McConkie explained, "The Eternal Giver of Gifts has special endowments of divine grace, special gifts and blessings for those who love and serve him with all their hearts. These gifts are freely offered to all men but are given to those only who meet the divine standard upon which their receipt is predicated" (A New Witness for the Articles of Faith, 358).

It is important to understand, however, that Moroni did not say these gifts were only for perfect followers, or unusually spiritually gifted followers, or doctrinally brilliant followers. He said True Followers, and in doing so identified a condition we all can achieve or at least aspire to, for following the Savior with a true and honest heart is something we are all capable of doing.

This is not to suggest that discipleship is easy, neither can it be intermittent. Some followers during Jesus' day reacted to His teachings with, "This is an hard saying; who can hear it?" (John 6:60), and subsequently "walked no more with him" (John 6:66).

Being a True Follower is an ongoing process. Everyone starts at a different place and has different obstacles and challenges with which to grapple, and most of us are not anywhere close to perfect. But being a disciple of Christ is not about being perfect—at least, not yet. It is about wanting to be a True Follower more than we want anything else.

What, then, is a True Follower?

The scriptures are filled with suggested characteristics. The qualities mentioned in the following pages are simply a few possible evidences of followership, or discipleship, offered with the hope that they will encourage you to search to know for yourself what true followership entails. Note that the verbs describing these attributes do not indicate that True Followers have "arrived" spiritually or achieved perfection, but that they are headed toward Christ rather than away from Him.

First, a True Follower is willing to walk away from the world.

We have already discussed the fact that it is dangerous to take counsel from anyone whose primary motive is building his or her own kingdom rather than the Lord's, and that the fundamental question we must ask ourselves is, who do we trust, and to whom are we listening, the world or the Lord?

Trusting in the arm of the flesh always has a downside. The Roman statesman Cicero said that "one does not have to believe everything one hears" (quoted in Panati, *Words to Live*

By, 41), which calls to mind one of Aesop's fables, "The Sick Lion":

"The lion king allowed word to circulate through the jungle that he was on his deathbed and wished all the animals of his kingdom to come to his cave to pay their respects—and hear the bequeaths from his last will and testament. Everyone would get a gift.

"The fox, who lived by his wits, was loath to enter the cave first. So he lingered near the entrance while the goat and the sheep and the calf ventured in to receive their bequeaths from the king of beasts.

"After a time, the lion appeared at the mouth of the cave looking remarkably fit. Sighed the fox to himself, A miraculous recovery!

"The lion saw the fox standing at a distance and called in a feeble bellow, patently fake, 'Come in and pay your respects, friend fox. My days are numbered.'

"'Please pardon me, Your Majesty,' replied the fox, 'but in your delicate condition, you shouldn't have to put up with crowds. So many tracks lead into your cave, and none lead away. Until some of your guests come out, I'll stay here in the open air'" (quoted in Panati, *Words to Live By*, 42).

The moral of the story is obvious: Just as the fox didn't believe the lion, you can't believe everything you hear. That can be tough to remember in today's world, where glib, smart, talented entertainers and communicators have made an art form of selling themselves and their philosophies. But, again, mortals make mistakes—some of which are innocent, some of which are not. And it can be difficult to tell the difference. Both taking counsel from man and doing things to be seen of man are spiritual dead-ends.

When we do our alms or pray or preach on street corners to be seen of man, we have our reward, a reward that is short-lived under the best of circumstances (see 3 Nephi 13:1–8). By contrast, gifts from above are infinite and eternal. The world cannot duplicate or even approximate the gifts our Father has for those who look first to follow His Son.

Second, a True Follower believes Jesus is the Christ, and is striving to increase his or her faith in Him.

There is a reason faith is the first principle of the gospel. It is a principle of power.

And yet, the daily realities of life can threaten our faith at times. C. S. Lewis had an interesting way of describing what sometimes happens even to believers:

> *The world cannot duplicate or even approximate the gifts our Father has for those who look first to follow His Son.*

"There are things, say in learning to swim or to climb, which look dangerous and aren't. Your instructor tells you it's safe. You have good reason from past experience to trust him. Perhaps you can even see for yourself . . . that it is safe. But the crucial question is, will you be able to go on believing this when you actually see the cliff edge below you or actually feel yourself unsupported in the water? You will have no *rational* grounds for disbelieving. It is your senses and your imagination that are going to attack belief. Here, as in the New Testament, the conflict is not between faith and reason but between faith and sight. . . . Our faith in Christ wavers not so much when real arguments come against it as when it *looks* improbable—when the whole world takes on the desolate *look* which really tells us much more about the state of our passions and even our digestion than about reality" (*The Quotable Lewis,* 207; emphasis in original).

It is our willingness to believe in the Savior—even when we cannot walk and talk with Him, and when we might feel that we aren't "worthy" of His help—that unleashes His power in our lives. As the Prophet Joseph taught, faith is both a "principle of action [and] of power also, in all intelligent beings, whether in heaven or on earth. . . . Had it not been for the principle of faith the worlds would never have been framed, neither would man have been formed of the dust. It is the principle by which Jehovah works, and through which he exercises power over all temporal as well as eternal things. Take this principle or attribute—for it is an attribute—from the Deity, and he would cease to exist. Who cannot see, that if God framed the worlds by faith, that it is by faith that he exercises power over them, and that faith is the principle of power?" (*Lectures on Faith,* 1:13, 16–17).

The dominant message of the writings and teachings of ancient prophets is that Jesus is the Christ, and that faith in Him is a principle of power.

The young Nephi was allowed to see what his father Lehi had seen in vision because he believed: "Blessed art thou,

Nephi," proclaimed the Spirit of the Lord, "because thou believest in the Son of the most high God; wherefore, thou shalt behold the things which thou hast desired" (1 Nephi 11:6). The brother of Jared saw the Lord because never had man come before Him "with such exceeding faith" (Ether 3:9). Joseph who was sold into Egypt, Abraham and Isaac, Rebekah, Alma the Younger and the Sons of Mosiah, Mormon and Moroni, Moses—the accounts of the fruits of their faith, and the faith of many others of the ancients, are countless.

Their examples all teach the same lesson: that God and His Son are all-powerful, and that when we have faith in Them— and when They trust us—we have access to Their power. When those who have greater authority than we (and to whom we often report our various stewardships) have confidence in us and trust us, they increasingly share with us their power. Nowhere is this principle more evident than in the way the Father and the Son interact with us.

Even when and if a True Follower doesn't believe in himself, he believes in the Lord. This may mean just being willing to experiment upon His word, even starting with the simple prayer, "Lord, I believe; help thou mine unbelief" (Mark 9:24). A True Follower is nonetheless striving to increase his faith in the Lord.

Third, a True Follower is humble enough to obey and repent.

Sin makes us stupid, and it costs a lot too—a lot of time, money, peace of mind, opportunity to progress, self-respect, integrity, virtue, and the trust of loved ones. Chapter Two elaborates on how crucial it is that we are humble enough to obey, and humble enough to repent when we make mistakes. Obedience is the way we show the Lord we're serious about Him.

Obedience is the way we show the Lord we're serious about Him.

Not long ago I attended a meeting where a member of the Quorum of the Twelve addressed a group of young adults. At one point, he invited them to ask questions. The questions focused on dating, marriage, careers, and finding their way in life. One young man raised his hand and stumbled around trying to find a delicate way to ask what it was like to be an Apostle. This wise and kind man said simply, "A day doesn't go by that I'm not aware that I need to be better."

His sincerity and humility in considering where he was along life's path taught all of us a lesson that day. A True Follower is humble.

Fourth, a True Follower is a diligent seeker.

Thomas Jefferson said: "I am a great believer in luck, and I find the harder I work the more I have of it" (in Panati, *Words to Live By*, 78).

True Followers work. They *do* things. The more they do, the better "luck"—or at least opportunities—they have. And they typically do things differently and more regularly than those who aren't engaged in true followership.

C. S. Lewis said that "the trouble is that relying on God has to begin all over again every day as if nothing had yet been done" (*The Quotable Lewis*, 156). This means making worship a central part of life. True Followers pray. They have some kind of regular pattern of scripture study. They don't "find time" to go to the temple, they set it as a priority first and work other things around it. They welcome the opportunity to fast as a regular way of humbling themselves, putting God first, seeking answers to prayers, and strengthening their connection to the Lord. They do these things not to check them off some kind of forced obedience checklist, but because they have learned to find answers and peace in the temple, in the scriptures, and through prayer and fasting—and these elements of devotion are woven into the fabric of their daily life rather than something done on Sunday or sporadically as needed. Righteous acts help define who they are.

True Followers diligently seek to know the Lord and His doctrine, to understand His will for them, to know how to handle the latest challenge or even the latest triumph, to find answers to questions or dilemmas, even doctrines, that confuse or trouble them. They do this not to comply with some unwritten code of behavior, but because they really do want to follow Jesus Christ. They want to understand His gospel, particularly how it applies to them. They want to have their lamps filled with testimony and faith so they're ready when the Bridegroom comes, but also so they're ready when doubt or conflict or trial descend, usually without warning (see Matthew 25:1–13).

We live in a connected world. When I was growing up, the only telephone in the house was on the kitchen wall attached to a cord. Today, in every country of the world, men and women, boys and girls, ride subways and jeepneys and bicycles with cell phones in hand, many of them sophisticated enough to send and receive calls, text messages, e-mail, and downloads any hour of the night or day. We want to be connected and go to extraordinary lengths and expense to be so.

Do we make even a fraction as much effort at connecting and staying connected with the heavens—with immersing ourselves in the Word of God and experiencing for ourselves its power, with seeking to learn the language of revelation and how to hear the voice of the Lord? The ultimate connection is conversing with our Father, in the name of Jesus Christ, through the ministering of the Holy Ghost. And that connection comes as a result of diligently, earnestly, steadily seeking, the reward for which is great: "For he that diligently seeketh shall find; and the mysteries of God shall be unfolded unto them, by the power of the Holy Ghost" (1 Nephi 10:19).

A mission president's wife shared this story of a young elder who struggled from the day he entered the mission field:

"Elder Smith [not his real name] has been out for five months and has wanted to go home since he arrived. He had a tremendous companion and they taught and baptized, but it didn't change his mind or heart. He would stand alone in the hall while other missionaries congregated at meetings. He said he had no one in the mission—no friends, no one close. And even worse, he told the mission president he didn't have a testimony, never had, and was only here because it had been so important to his parents. Day after day he just tried to get through it.

"The president worked with him, counseled him, and did

182

everything he could think of to help him grasp the significance of this mission experience in his life. Nothing seemed to help. Then the president felt prompted to extend this elder's study time by one hour a day. 'Read the Book of Mormon and pray for a witness,' he told the elder.

"Elder Smith was the last person I expected to see stand to bear his testimony in this particular zone conference. 'I have never borne my testimony before without being forced to do it,' he began. 'I've never had a testimony.' You can imagine the silence in the room. 'Many of you don't know me. I have always been chosen last for any athletic team. It's just always been that way. But it doesn't matter anymore, because I know. I know,' he said. 'I know that the gospel is true and I know the Book of Mormon is God's word. I know,' he said again. He explained that he had been studying and praying and had received a witness in his heart.

"I sat stunned. Elder Smith had been on my death watch. And now, he was addressing half the mission and stirring our hearts with his testimony. He is a changed man. He has a smile on his face and an arm around any elder who needs a boost. He has become a missionary."

He had also become a True Follower, the result of diligently studying the Word of God.

Quoting Isaiah, Nephi taught the profound truth that "my people are gone into captivity, because they have no knowledge. . . . Therefore, hell hath enlarged herself" (2 Nephi 15:13–14). Those in spiritual bondage are those who have no knowledge. There is nothing more important than actually knowing what we believe and what the gospel of Jesus Christ entails.

Information precedes inspiration. The payoff for seeking spiritual knowledge is guaranteed: "For *every one* that asketh, receiveth; and he that seeketh, findeth" (3 Nephi 14:8; emphasis added).

Fifth, a True Follower desires to follow Christ.

It is significant that when Joseph went into the grove to pray, he knelt and offered up "the desires of [his] heart to God" (JS–H 1:15).

We pay attention to and spend time on those things and people we really care about. We seek after that which we really desire. Hence the reason Alma counseled his son Helaman to "cry unto God for all thy support; yea, let all thy doings be unto the Lord, and whithersoever thou goest let it be in the Lord; yea, let all thy thoughts be directed unto the Lord; yea, let the affections of thy heart be placed upon the Lord forever" (Alma 37:36). Alma was imploring his son to put the Lord first, to place his affection on the Lord rather than anything else, knowing that where our hearts are, there will our energy and effort and time be also.

There is nothing more important than actually knowing what we believe and what the gospel of Jesus Christ entails.

Thus, if we can "no more than desire to believe, let this desire work in [us]" (Alma 32:27), for desiring to do good, to seek after truth and light, to follow the Lord will lead to an

enlargement of our souls and our understanding, to joy in the
fruits of the gospel (see Alma 32:28).

None of us is perfect. We make mistakes every day. But we
can become perfect in our desire to follow Christ. And He
judges all men "according to their works, according to the
desire of their hearts" (D&C 137:9).

*Sixth, a True Follower has the sense that, despite imperfections
and weaknesses, his or her life is in harmony with the Lord's will.*

The Prophet Joseph taught that
three things are necessary for a person to have true faith: first, he or
she must know and believe that
God exists; second, he must have a
correct idea of His character, perfec-
tions, and attributes; and third, he
must have the assurance that one's
course of life is according to and
harmonious with God's mind and
will (see *Lectures on Faith*, 3). Said
he: "Such was, and always will be,
the situation of the saints of God,

> *None of us is perfect.*
>
> *We make mistakes every*
>
> *day. But we can become*
>
> *perfect in our desire to*
>
> *follow Christ.*

that unless they have an actual knowledge that the course they
are pursuing is according to the will of God they will grow
weary in their minds, and faint" (*Lectures on Faith*, 6:4).

Even if a True Follower's life is following a pattern he or she
would not have chosen and may not even like very much, if
that person knows his life is in harmony with the Lord's will,
he can keep going and even progressing. Further, when our
Father asks one of His children to do something he never saw

himself doing and probably doesn't want to do, a True Follower has the faith necessary to reconcile himself to the will of the Lord and go forward—praying there will be either a lamb in the thicket, as Abraham experienced with Isaac on Mt. Moriah, or unexpected protection and safety, as with Daniel in the lion's den.

Seventh, a True Follower seeks to be more pure.

The prophet Jacob spoke to the pure in heart, promising that the Lord would console them in their afflictions and plead their cause with the Father, adding: "O all ye that are pure in heart, lift up your heads and receive the pleasing word of God, and feast upon his love; for ye may, if your minds are firm, forever" (Jacob 3:1–2).

As outlined in the first chapter, purity—of heart, mind, desires, motives, body, actions, and language—is key to learning the language of revelation. It is a key to having the Spirit always with us. It is key to being endowed with power.

We won't become perfect in this life. But we can become steadily, increasingly pure even as the world becomes steadily, increasingly polluted. And that distinction among True Followers will increasingly attract the attention of those who are "kept from the truth because they know not where to find it" (D&C 123:12).

One vitally important facet of life Satan has successfully managed to contaminate on an almost unlimited scale is that of sexual purity. He has turned what the Lord intended to be the most sublime and pure expression of love between a husband and a wife into something casual and even tawdry—an impulse to be satisfied at all costs (and too often despite the moral and spiritual cost). He has attempted, and in far too many arenas succeeded, in reducing sexual intimacy to its most selfish, base, and degraded form.

How offensive sexual immorality must be to our Father, who not only gave husband and wife the privilege of expressing their affection in a manner that bespeaks complete union and oneness, but extended to them also the high privilege of pro-creation. And creation, including procreation, is one of the things that makes God, God.

Elder Dallin H. Oaks taught that "the power to create mor-tal life is the most exalted power God has given his children. Its use was mandated in the first commandment, but another important commandment was given to forbid its misuse. The emphasis we place on the law of chastity is explained by our understanding of the purpose of our procreative powers in the accomplishment of God's plan. The expression of our procre-ative powers is pleasing to God, but he has commanded that this be confined within the relationship of marriage. . . . Outside the bonds of marriage, all uses of the procreative power are to one degree or another a sinful degrading and perversion of the most divine attribute of men and women" ("The Great Plan of Happiness," 74).

It becomes clear in the temple how important purity is, and particularly sexual purity, for living that law is required if a man or woman is to have any hope of living anything other than a telestial life.

Anything filthy, base, or degrading is inspired by Lucifer. Anything pure is from the Lord.

When the Savior's twelve Nephite disciples were transfigured, the "light of [the Savior's] countenance did shine upon them, and behold they were as white as the countenance and also the garments of Jesus" (3 Nephi 19:25). Jesus responded with a prayer of gratitude: "Father, I thank thee that thou hast purified those whom I have chosen, because of their faith" (3 Nephi 19:28).

Purity is something we can increasingly achieve. Purity is key to drawing upon the power of the Lord. Purity is always a characteristic of a True Follower of Jesus Christ.

Eighth, a True Follower looks like a True Follower.

Purity is an essential characteristic of someone endeavoring to follow the Savior, and that purity can actually be observed in the way a True Follower looks, acts, behaves, and even dresses.

A few years ago, a friend and I made the mistake of going to Disney World in Orlando, Florida, during July. Florida in July is hot, hot, hot—with the heat being exceeded only by the humidity. Most days it was nearly 100 degrees with 100 percent humidity. It was miserable!

Purity is an essential characteristic of someone endeavoring to follow the Savior, and that purity can actually be observed in the way a True Follower looks, acts, behaves, and even dresses.

Extreme heat seems to inspire the most interesting kind of attire—or lack thereof—and after a while my friend and I started playing a game. As we walked around Disney World, maneuvering among the thousands of guests who were also dealing with the extreme heat, we started looking for others who looked, by their clothing, to be endowed temple-goers. This focus on what the masses were wearing was enlightening. There were many people—particularly women, I'm sorry to say—immodestly dressed. There were also lots of people modestly dressed by the world's standards but whose clothing indicated they were not temple-goers. And there were a few—and I mean a *handful*—of individuals walking around that immense park dressed in a manner that could have accommodated the temple garment.

You can pick True Followers out in a crowd, any crowd. They stand out because they look different from the masses. They look like True Followers because they show respect for the covenants they've made and a sanctity for the divine nature of their bodies.

President Gordon B. Hinckley declared that "if we are to hold up this Church as an ensign to the nations and a light to the world, we must take on more of the luster of the life of Christ individually and in our own personal circumstances" ("An Ensign to the Nations, a Light to the World," 84).

Surely the luster of our lives includes the way we look, meaning the way we take care of and present ourselves. This is not to encourage or suggest extreme makeovers with all of their nipping and tucking and implanting, basically reconstructing various parts of our bodies. I am talking about the way we take care of our bodies, and the way we present ourselves to others.

Joseph Smith taught that "we came to this earth that we might have a body and present it pure before God in the Celestial Kingdom. The great principle of happiness consists in having a body. The Devil has no body, and herein is his punishment" (Ehat and Cook, eds., *Words of Joseph Smith*, 60). Satan has no body, and never will. It is one of the reasons he's miserable, and always will be. It is also one of the reasons he inspires every conceivable form of bodily abuse and misuse. He doesn't want those who have bodies to realize that receiving a body is part of God's great plan of happiness. He doesn't want us to understand that our bodies were created in the express image of our Father. Or that our bodies house our spirits.

It was the Savior who first compared His body to a temple (see John 2:21). The Apostle Paul was more explicit with the people in the wicked city of Corinth: "Know ye not that ye are the temple of God, and that the Spirit of God dwelleth in you? If any man defile the temple of God, him shall God destroy; for the temple of God is holy, which temple ye are" (1 Corinthians 3:16–17).

The Father and the Son have bodies of "flesh and bones as tangible as man's" (D&C 130:22). At least one element of the condescension of Jesus Christ was His willingness to take upon Himself a mortal body and subject that body to physical temptation. The Savior's holiness, in part, is a result of overcoming temptations related to the body.

While the human body is subject to temptations of the

flesh as well as pain and illness, it also contains within it the power to create life. It is, by that fact alone, a sacred and holy temple. It deserves to be treated with reverence, just as we would respect any temple that houses the Spirit of the Lord.

Elder LeGrand Richards of the Quorum of the Twelve said this: "I want to tell you right now that the body is the tabernacle of the Holy Spirit. My daddy [George Franklin Richards, formerly President of the Quorum of the Twelve] taught me that the choice spirits of heaven might have the right to choose the lineage through which they are born, and if you will keep your bodies clean inside and out, the spirit of the Lord can dwell in you. Then you can become worthy to receive the chosen and choice spirits of heaven. . . . You can just imagine that the choice spirits of heaven might want to know that they are coming into the lives of clean men and clean women" (BYU *Speeches of the Year*, 1963, 10).

The Savior's holiness, in part, is a result of overcoming temptations related to the body.

. Our bodies are one of our Father's greatest gifts to us, and yet they also seem to create the most temptations. One of the difficulties of mortality is learning to submit our bodies, our thoughts, and our desires not only to the Lord's will but to behavior prescribed by Him. As we subject ourselves to Him, He is more able to bless us and to gradually change our very natures so that we are like Him—which is a far cry from what we see almost everywhere we look.

The defilement and degradation of people's bodies is everywhere to be seen today. Walk through any airport, or just about any public place, for that matter, and you'll see people whom you could have seen only in a carnival just a few years back. Earrings in noses, ears, lips, cheeks, eyebrows, and basically any bodily protrusion. Tattoos covering massive parts of the body. Slovenly and unkempt dress. Brazenly immodest clothing that is nothing more than underwear masquerading as everyday apparel. Walk through any public place, and all this—and much more—can be seen.

Not long ago I spoke to a gathering of young adults in a midwestern city. I love young adults and am convinced they are a pivotal generation in the history of this dispensation. They are brighter, smarter, and more faithful than any generation this world has ever seen. And they're also highly susceptible to the machinations of men and the trends of today. After the message, a gorgeous young woman approached me. It would have been impossible not to notice what she was wearing, because there was so little of it. She thanked me for the message and said the Spirit had spoken to her and told her what she needed to do at this point in her life. It is always a relief to hear that comment, because it is clear then that the Spirit has done the teaching, and not me. I couldn't help but hope, however, for her sake, that she had had the impression that it was time to change her wardrobe, because her clothing was selling both her body and her spirit short.

Said Elder Jeffrey R. Holland: "Modesty in appearance is *always* in fashion. Our standards are *not* socially negotiable. . . .

Avoid clothing that is too tight, too short, or improperly revealing in any manner, including bare midriffs. . . . Choose your clothing the way you would choose your friends—in both cases choose that which improves you and would give you confidence standing in the presence of God. Good friends would never embarrass you, demean you, or exploit you. Neither should your clothing" ("To Young Women," 29).

Last year I traveled to England with my two sisters and five nieces between the ages of fifteen and eighteen. A couple of months before leaving, in an effort to talk with the girls about the kind of clothing they might take with them abroad, we held a family home evening for our extended family in which we reviewed the talks on modesty Elder Jeffrey R. Holland of the Quorum of the Twelve and Sister Susan Tanner, Young Women general president, had delivered in the October 2005 general conference.

The home evening in question happened to fall on Easter Sunday. After reviewing the principles from these two classic addresses, I asked my nieces and nephews why, on Easter Sunday, I would choose to give a lesson on modesty. "In other words," I clarified, "what do modesty and the Savior have to do with one another?"

There was a long pause, and then my youngest niece raised her hand. "Because how we dress shows how we feel about the Savior. Right?"

She couldn't have been more right.

How we dress, meaning not how expensive but how appropriate and modest our clothing is; how we treat the magnificent gift of our bodies, the temples that house our spirits; the kind of language we use; and whether or not we are virtuous and clean in everything from how we handle ourselves to what we wear—all are indications of how we feel about the Savior because they are indications of whether or not we are trying to live as True Followers.

That trip to England last summer proved to be delightful and enlightening. Everywhere we went, heads turned as our five teenage girls walked by. Yes, they are darling—but in terms of God-given physical features, perhaps not markedly different from many teenage girls. But heads turned, I believe, because these girls looked so different from most other young women walking the streets. They were cute, but even more, there was a wholesomeness, a cleanliness, and a kind of fashionable modesty about them. And most of all, they were filled with light—the light that comes from having the Holy Ghost present.

Our bodies are temples. Gaining a body was a great and important step that made us even more like our Father.

Our bodies are temples. Gaining a body was a great and important step that made us even more like our Father. Respect for that body is a sign of a True Follower. True followers *look like* followers of Jesus Christ.

Ninth, a True Follower understands that some things and some places are holy.

One of the challenges of life in a telestial sphere is learning to recognize those things that are holy and deserve to be treated with both respect and reverence. This can be challenging when Satan is trying to reduce everything holy into something a little less so. He wants to ruin anything and everything sacred. In some eras and among some cultures there were—and in some cases still are—clear distinctions between things of the world and things of God, between the formal and the informal, between things of a carnal, self-indulgent nature and those that are holy. Today in many cultures those distinctions have been blurred.

As an example, marriage is a sacrament, an ordinance of the highest order. It is holy to the Lord. And yet, by many, marriage is seen as something even less binding than a legal contract, something to be tried but not bound by.

There are other things, events, and places that are holy.

The Sabbath is holy, as we learned when the Lord thundered from Mt. Sinai for His chosen people to "remember the sabbath day, to keep it holy" (Exodus 20:8). Our company recently engaged the services of a first-rate young attorney who happened to be Jewish and who religiously honored *Shabbat*, the Jewish Sabbath observed from sunset on Friday until sunset on Saturday. From the precise time of sundown on Friday until sundown on Saturday, he wouldn't work, couldn't be reached by phone or e-mail, and wouldn't travel—it was holy. More than once we were on a conference call with him late on Friday afternoon when he would say, "I can talk for nine more minutes, and then I'm done for twenty-four hours." And at the nine-minute mark, he was gone. We used to tease him that it was tough for a Jewish attorney with LDS clients to get much done on the weekend, but happily so. Ironically, his strict reverence and observance of *Shabbat* increased not only our respect for him but our view of him professionally. If he took such great care to honor the Lord precisely, it seemed likely that he would take great care of us as his client. And he did.

We might well ask ourselves if we are as careful to honor the Sabbath as my Jewish friend. Sometimes appearance is not deceiving, for at times it *looks* as though some have taken seriously a banner that hung for several months outside a New York City cathedral: "Come dressed in your Sunday worst."

Elder Holland appealed to the women of the Church to examine the way they dress for Sabbath day worship. Said he: "We used to speak of 'best dress' and 'Sunday dress,' and maybe we should do so again. In any case, from ancient times to modern, we have always been invited to present our best selves inside and out when entering the house of the Lord—and a dedicated LDS chapel is a 'house of the Lord.' Our clothing or footwear need never be expensive, . . . but neither should it appear that we are on our way to the beach. When we come to worship the God and Father of us all and to partake of the sacrament symbolizing the Atonement of Jesus Christ, we should be as comely and respectful, as dignified and appropriate as we can be. *We should be recognizable in appearance as well as in behavior that we truly are disciples of Christ*" ("To Young Women," 29; emphasis added).

Today's casual society has produced an informality that has now crept into nearly every aspect of our culture, including, sadly, even Sabbath day worship. Particularly among women, there is a regrettable tendency to wear into the chapel and then partake of the emblems of the sacrament in the same clothing one might wear to the mall or the park or even, as Elder Holland suggested, to the beach.

What is wrong with this? Isn't it enough just to show up at church?

The chapel is an ordinance room. What takes place there every Sabbath day is an ordinance in which we have the privilege of presenting ourselves before the Lord and committing once again to follow and serve Him. If we suddenly received notice from the prophet that the Lord would make a special appearance in our sacrament meeting next Sunday, it would be no different in terms of the covenant we are renewing. Surely few among us would kneel and present ourselves before the Savior wearing flip-flops or even, dare I say it, denim.

Today's casual society has produced an informality that has now crept into nearly every aspect of our culture, including, sadly, even our Sabbath day worship.

The Sabbath day is a holy day, set aside to encourage us to rest from our labors but more importantly to worship the Risen Lord. Do we reverence that day, and would our reverence be apparent to others?

There are other specific places on earth—at last count, 124

of them—where *Holiness to the Lord* is actually engraved on the exterior.

Not terribly long ago, I had just finished an endowment session and entered the celestial room of the temple when an eager woman, anxious to say hello, grabbed my arm and began to tell me a story. I'm sure her intentions were only to be friendly and welcoming. But I had just spent an hour and a half in the marvelous learning environment afforded by the endowment, culminating in one of the holiest places on earth, eager not to talk with other people but to worship the Lord. I've had and observed countless experiences when such worship has been interrupted.

The temple, and certainly the celestial room, was not designed as a meet-and-greet location. Lovely opportunities to welcome those we love or are grateful to be united with can happily take place outside. The ordinances of the temple are holy and bless us with the privilege of learning how to part the veil and communicate with the heavens.

There are other places, times, and things that are holy.

The administration of the sacrament is a time of holiness.

Sincere prayer can be a time of holiness.

All things and places are not created equal—not in the eyes of the Lord. And over time, True Followers become more able to identify times and places the Lord intended to be holy, and to learn that we remain holy by pushing the telestial nature of our lives aside and treating such places with reverence and respect.

Tenth: a True Follower is a leader, and in order to lead, one must first learn to follow.

War sometimes forces those involved to emerge as leaders. Referring to England's role in World War II, Winston Churchill said in a speech to the House of Commons on the occasion of his eightieth birthday, "It was a nation and race dwelling all round the globe that had the lion heart. I had the luck to be called upon to give the roar" (Best, *Churchill: A Study in Greatness*, 183).

An old Arabic proverb says that an army of sheep led by a lion will defeat an army of lions led by a sheep. True Followers who have heard the voice of the Good Shepherd and are following Him as His sheep have also the obligation and the ability to lead out as lions, with energy and strength, in opposing anything and anyone who opposes Him.

In today's world, there are too many good people with no conviction, and too many evil people filled with conviction. The world is crying out for true leadership—which is why these are the days in which a true leader wants to live, for the opportunities to change lives and even destinies are endless. If it is true, as C. S. Lewis wrote, that "there is no neutral ground in the universe: every square inch, every split second, is claimed by God and counterclaimed by Satan" (*The Quotable Lewis*, 260), then never has there been a

> In today's world, there are too many good people with no conviction, and too many evil people filled with conviction.

greater need for men and women who know what they believe, who speak and defend truth, who stand by their convictions, and who lead others to do likewise.

True Followers make the best leaders. True Followers are men and women the Lord will endow with power to assist Him in His mighty work.

The characteristics of True Followers of Christ noted in this chapter are just a beginning. The scriptures are filled with examples of other attributes of those who wish, above all else, to be disciples of Jesus Christ. Our challenge is to seek those qualities out, to contemplate them, and to work, day by day, here a little and there a little, to add those virtues to our lives.

The answer to every problem, every challenge, every worry, every heartache this life can pose is to have a testimony that Jesus is the Christ, that His gospel has been restored, and that the gospel is filled with power available to those who qualify for and seek after that power. Knowing for ourselves that Jesus Christ is our Redeemer and Savior, our Advocate with the Father, we must learn to follow Him without reservation.

And the key to all of this is becoming a True Follower of Jesus Christ.

Again, quoting Churchill during the darkest days of World War II: "Come then: let us to the task, to the battle, to the toil—each to our part, each to our station. Fill the armies, rule the air, pour out the munitions, strangle the U-boats, sweep the mines, plough the land, build the ships, guard the streets, succour the wounded, uplift the downcast, and honour the brave. Let us go forward together in all parts of the Empire, in all parts of the Island. There is not a week, nor a day, nor an hour to lose" (Best, *Churchill: A Study in Greatness*, 168).

Likewise, in this great latter-day battle, the Lord needs every True Follower to step forward—in every part of His kingdom—to draw upon and use every gift and endowment he or she has been given. There isn't a week, a day, an hour to lose.

Elder Jeffrey R. Holland declared that "something is going to be asked of this dispensation that's never been asked before. Those of this dispensation must be ready to present the Church of the Lamb, to the Lamb, and when that happens we must be looking and acting like His Church" (*Church News*, February 17, 2007).

In other words, we must be a Church of True Followers—followers who know, for sure, that this is The Church of Jesus Christ,

—that every spiritual privilege we have emanates from Him and His gospel,

—that His gospel contains His priesthood, the priesthood after the order of the Son of God,

—that because of Him, we may receive the gift and power of the Holy Ghost,

—that because of Him, there is power in the Word, because He is the Word,

—that because of Him, we may be healed, strengthened, forgiven, purified, delivered, sanctified, and eventually made perfect,

—that because of Him, we may be endowed with power in the House of the Lord.

The past couple of years have been more rigorous spiritually, and emotionally, and even physically than any I can remember. For one reason or another, virtually every area of my life has been affected and in some fashion challenged.

I've been brought face to face with my greatest fears, forced to confront my greatest weaknesses and waves of disappointment, burdened with suffocating pressure, and experienced some of my greatest heartaches. Answers to prayer haven't always come quickly, and some issues of great concern and constant pleading even still remain unresolved.

Sometimes life is just plain old hard.

But hard is not necessarily bad . . . it's just hard. And during intense times, we sometimes grow and learn the most. Despite the disappointments and challenges—and often because of them—there are some things I know today better than I knew before. There are some things that simply cannot be taken from me.

During intense times, we sometimes grow and learn the most.

I know that God is our Father, and that He is serious about us. He is serious about our becoming as He is and fully intends us to return home. That is why He created a plan and gave us His Son, even His Firstborn and Only Begotten Son in the flesh, so that we could become who we have the potential to become.

I know that Jesus is the Christ, and that He can and will

forgive and redeem us. Not only that, but He can sanctify us, strengthen us, deliver us from everything from oppression to fear, and enable us to do and endure things we could never do or endure on our own. I know that He will carry burdens too heavy for us to carry, that He is filled with mercy and love, that He is quick to forgive when we repent, that He stands by us even when we don't do as well as we know how. And I know that He can heal hearts, minds, emotions, and afflictions. And that He does.

I know that the heavens are open, that the veil is thin, that angels minister to us, that the Lord will teach us things that can be learned only through and by the Spirit, that the Holy Ghost is both a gift and a power, and that the privilege of receiving revelation through Him is an unspeakable gift.

I know that our Father wants to give us everything and teach us everything.

I know that there is power in the doctrines of the gospel of Jesus Christ, that there is power in the ordinances of the priesthood, that the priesthood is in very fact the power of God delegated to man on earth, and that every worthy man and woman has access to that power.

I know that the Father bestows His multitude of gifts upon those who follow His Son, and that the only sustaining source of peace, hope, strength, and love is in Jesus Christ.

I know that the greatest way to worship our Father is by following His Son.

And I know that the Father and the Son share Their power

with True Followers who qualify for and learn to access that privilege.

The message of the gospel of Jesus Christ is clear: God wants a powerful people.

SOURCES CITED

Ballard, M. Russell. "The Greatest Generation of Missionaries." *Ensign*, November 2002, 46–49.

Best, Geoffrey. *Churchill: A Study in Greatness*. London: Hambledon and London, 2001.

Cannadine, David, and Winston Churchill. *Blood, Toil, Tears and Sweat: The Speeches of Winston Churchill*. London: Penguin Books, 1990.

Cannon, George Q. *Gospel Truth: Discourses and Writings of George Q. Cannon*. Edited by Jerreld L. Newquist. Salt Lake City: Deseret Book, 1987.

Clark, J. Reuben, Jr. "Our Wives and Our Mothers in the Eternal Plan." *Relief Society Magazine*, December 1946, 799–801.

Dew, Sheri. *Go Forward with Faith: The Biography of Gordon B. Hinckley*. Salt Lake City: Deseret Book, 1996.

Ehat, Andrew F., and Lyndon W. Cook, eds. *The Words of Joseph Smith*. Provo, Utah: BYU Religious Studies Center, 1980.

Eyring, Henry B. "The Power of Teaching Doctrine." *Ensign*, May 1999, 73–75.

———. "Spiritual Preparedness: Start Early and Be Steady." *Ensign*, November 2005, 37–40.

"The Family: A Proclamation to the World." *Ensign*, November 1995, 102.

Faust, James E. "The Forces That Will Save Us." *Ensign*, January 2007, 4–9.

Federer, William J. *America's God and Country*. St. Louis: Amerisearch, 2000.

Hafen, Bruce C. *The Broken Heart*. Salt Lake City: Deseret Book, 1989.

Hales, Robert D. "Preparations for the Restoration and the Second Coming: 'My Hand Shall Be over Thee.'" *Ensign*, November 2005, 88–92.

Hinckley, Gordon B. "As One Who Loves the Prophet." In Susan Easton Black and Charles D. Tate Jr., eds. *Joseph Smith: The Prophet, the Man*. Provo, Utah: BYU Religious Studies Center, 1993.

———. "The Dawning of a Brighter Day." *Ensign*, May 2004, 81–84.

———. "An Ensign to the Nations, a Light to the World," *Ensign*, November 2003, 82–85.

———. "The Great Things Which God Has Revealed." *Ensign*, May 2005, 80–83.

———. "Joseph Smith Jr.—Prophet of God, Mighty Servant." *Ensign*, December 2005, 2, 4–6.

———. "Personal Worthiness to Exercise the Priesthood." *Ensign*, May 2002, 52–54, 59.

Holland, Jeffrey R., "To Young Women." *Ensign*, November 2005, 28–30.

Journal of Discourses. 26 vols. London: Latter-day Saints' Book Depot, 1854–86.

Kimball, Spencer W. *Faith Precedes the Miracle*. Salt Lake City: Deseret Book, 1972.

———. "The Role of Righteous Women." *Ensign*, November 1979, 102–4.

———. *The Teachings of Spencer W. Kimball*. Edited by Edward L. Kimball. Salt Lake City: Bookcraft, 1985.

Lewis, C. S. *Mere Christianity*. San Francisco: HarperSan-Francisco, 2001.

———. *The Quotable Lewis*. Edited by Wayne Martindale and Jerry Root. Wheaton, Ill.: Tyndale House, 1989.

Maxwell, Neal A. *We Will Prove Them Herewith*. Salt Lake City: Deseret Book, 1982.

McConkie, Bruce R. "Be Valiant in the Fight of Faith." *Ensign*, November 1974, 33–35.

———. "The Doctrine of the Priesthood." *Ensign*, May 1982, 32–34.

———. *The Millennial Messiah*. Salt Lake City: Deseret Book, 1982.

———. *A New Witness for the Articles of Faith*. Salt Lake City: Deseret Book, 1985.

———. *The Promised Messiah*. Salt Lake City: Deseret Book, 1978.

———. "The Ten Blessings of the Priesthood." *Ensign*, November 1977, 33–35.

Oaks, Dallin H. "The Great Plan of Happiness," *Ensign*, November 1993, 72–75.

Packer, Boyd K. "Little Children." *Ensign*, November 1986, 16–18.

———. "What Every Elder Should Know—and Every Sister as Well: A Primer on Principles of Priesthood Government," *Ensign*, February 1993, 7–13.

Panati, Charles. *Words to Live By: The Origins of Conventional Wisdom and Commonsense Advice*. New York: Penguin, 1999.

Proctor, Scot Facer, and Maurine Jensen Proctor. *Autobiography of Parley P. Pratt,* revised and enhanced edition. Salt Lake City: Deseret Book, 2000.

Roberts, B. H. *A Comprehensive History of The Church of Jesus Christ of Latter-day Saints, Century One.* 6 vols. Salt Lake City: Deseret News Press, 1930.

Smith, Joseph. *History of the Church of Jesus Christ of Latter-day Saints.* Edited by B. H. Roberts. 2d ed. rev. 7 vols. Salt Lake City: The Church of Jesus Christ of Latter-day Saints, 1932–51.

———. *Lectures on Faith.* Salt Lake City: Deseret Book, 1985.

———. *Teachings of the Prophet Joseph Smith.* Selected and arranged by Joseph Fielding Smith. Salt Lake City: Deseret Book, 1976.

Smith, Joseph Fielding. *Doctrines of Salvation.* 3 vols. Compiled by Bruce R. McConkie. Salt Lake City: Bookcraft, 1954–56.

———. *Elijah: The Prophet and His Mission.* Salt Lake City: Deseret Book, 1957.

———. "Magnifying Our Callings in the Priesthood," *Improvement Era,* June 1970, 65–66.

———. *Take Heed to Yourselves!* Salt Lake City: Deseret Book, 1966.

Talmage, James E. "The Eternity of Sex," *Young Woman's Journal,* October 1914, 602–3.

———. *The House of the Lord.* Salt Lake City: Deseret Book, 1968.

———. *Jesus the Christ.* Salt Lake City: Deseret Book, 1983.

Taylor, John. *The Gospel Kingdom.* Salt Lake City: Bookcraft, 1987.

Welch, John W., ed. *Opening the Heavens: Accounts of Divine Manifestations, 1820–1844.* Provo, Utah: BYU Press, and Salt Lake City: Deseret Book, 2005.

Widtsoe, John A. *Priesthood and Church Government*. Salt Lake City: Deseret Book, 1939.

———. *Evidences and Reconciliations*. Arranged by G. Homer Durham. Salt Lake City: Bookcraft, 1960.

Wood, Robert S. *The Complete Christian*. Salt Lake City: Deseret Book, 2007.

Young, Brigham. *Discourses of Brigham Young*. Selected and arranged by John A. Widtsoe. Salt Lake City: Deseret Book, 1954.

INDEX

Revelation: language of, 34–35;
Spencer W. Kimball on
continued, 55; given to Joseph
Smith, 117–20; scriptures act as
conduit for, 124
Richards, LeGrand, on bodies and
spirits, 191
Righteousness, Robert S. Wood on
trials and, 131
Ripples, 19–20

Sabbath day, 195–97
Sacrifice, 131–32
Salzburg, Austria, 84–85
Sanctification, 45–46
Satan: God understands, 23;
compared to snake, 23–24;
Moses rebukes, 24–26; power of,
26–28, 126–28; nature and
attack methods of, 102–11; is
father of contention, 123–24;
attack on priesthood by, 159–60;
sexual immorality and, 186–88;
bodies and, 190
Scriptures: power of God in, 28–34;
examples of faith in, 50–51,
178–79; examples of backing up
in, 67–72; act as conduit for
revelation, 124
Sealing: priesthood and, 150–51;
John A. Widtsoe on priesthood
and, 156
Seeking: accessing power of God
by, 54–55; early, 82–83; Jesus
Christ, 82–87
Sexual purity, 186–88
Sheep, 199
"Sick Lion, The," 176–77
Sin, happiness and, 53–54
Smith, Emma, on translation of
Book of Mormon, 125–26
Smith, Joseph: on influence of

Satan, 27; on Book of Mormon,
34; on purity of women, 43; on
returning to God, 74;
importance of having testimony
of, 114; has First Vision, 115–17;
revelations given to, 117–20;
foreordination of, 120–23; prays
to overcome contention,
123–24; finds revelation
through scriptures, 124;
exercises faith to access power of
God, 124–26; overcomes power
of Satan, 126–28; weakness and
simplicity of, 128–29; trials and
persecution of, 129–32; critics
of, 132–34; learned line upon
line, 134–36; influence and
power of testimony of, 136; on
Melchizedek Priesthood, 148; on
endless lives, 150; on faith, 178;
on bodies, 190
Smith, Joseph Fielding: on
returning to Heavenly Father,
49–50; on priesthood and
women, 149–50
Smith, Joseph, Sr., moves family to
New York, 121–22
Snakes, 23–24
Sodom and Gomorrah, latter days
compared to, 10
Spirits, LeGrand Richards on
bodies and, 191
Spiritual privileges, 56
Spiritual progress: stalling, 65–66;
backing up during, 72–75
Storms, being prepared for, 83–84
Street lamp, 61–65

Talmage, James E.: on faith, 51; on
priesthood and women, 151
Taylor, John: on Holy Ghost as
source of happiness, 34; on
visions of Joseph Smith, 118–19;

ABOUT THE AUTHOR

Sheri Dew is a native of Ulysses, Kansas, and a graduate of Brigham Young University. She served as second counselor in the Relief Society general presidency from 1997 to 2002. In March 2003 the White House appointed her a member of the U.S. Delegation to the Commission on the Status of Women at the United Nations. She also serves as a member of the National Advisory Council for both the Marriott School of Management and the BYU School of Social Sciences, as well as a member of the President's Leadership Council for BYU—Hawaii.

In 2002, Sheri Dew became president and CEO of Deseret Book Company. She is the author of several bestselling books, including the biographies of President Gordon B. Hinckley and President Ezra Taft Benson.